Constantine

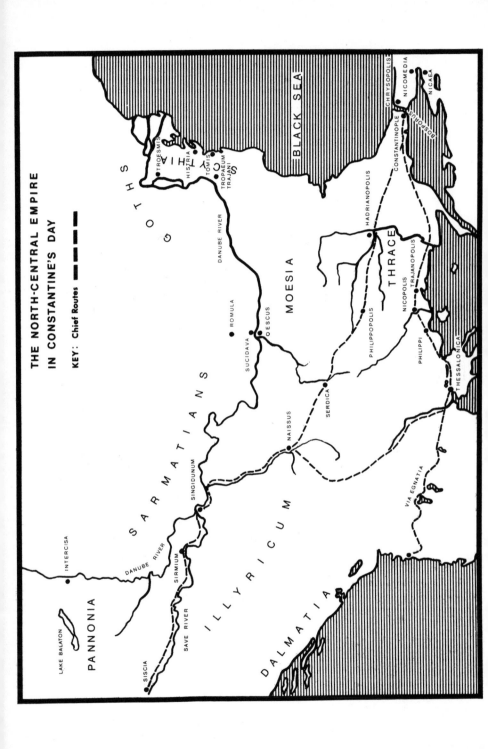

THE NORTH-CENTRAL EMPIRE
IN CONSTANTINE'S DAY

KEY: Chief Routes ▬ ▬ ▬

PANNONIA

LAKE BALATON

INTERCISA

DANUBE RIVER

SISCIA

SAVE RIVER

SIRMIUM

SINGIDUNUM

S A R M A T I A N S

G O T H S

TROESMIS
HISTRIA
TOMIS
CALLATIS
TROPAEUM
TRAJANI

S C Y T H I A

DANUBE RIVER

ROMULA

SUCIDAVA

OESCUS

M O E S I A

NAISSUS

SERDICA

PHILIPPOPOLIS

HADRIANOPOLIS

T H R A C E

NICOPOLIS

TRAJANOPOLIS

PHILIPPI

THESSALONICA

VIA EGNATIA

CONSTANTINOPLE

CHRYSOPOLIS

BOSPORUS

NICOMEDIA

NICAEA

BLACK SEA

I L L Y R I C U M

D A L M A T I A

Crosscurrents in World History

Constantine

by Ramsay MacMullen

WEIDENFELD AND NICOLSON
5 Winsley Street London WI

Books by Ramsay MacMullen

CONSTANTINE

SOLDIER AND CIVILIAN
IN THE LATER ROMAN EMPIRE

ENEMIES OF THE ROMAN ORDER: TREASON,
UNREST, AND ALIENATION
IN THE EMPIRE

Table of Contents

Illustrations

I

THE ROLE IS SET

The road that mounts the Capitoline hill in Rome today, shaking off its curves, at the top opens out on the Piazza del Campidoglio. In the center is a life-size equestrian statue of Marcus Aurelius. The horse strides vibrantly through the air, filled with strength; its rider—bearded, prim, slightly exophthalmic—seems quite out of place on its back. He is too unheroic, too civilian; too well known to us, perhaps. We know his correspondence with his tutor Fronto, how each surmounted a headache, a cough, or the ague, the delight they shared in the refinements of rhetoric. "If you are ever tied up in perpetual business," Fronto advises him on the duties of his office, "and thus lack the time to compose an oration, have you not derived support from certain hurried but profitable recreations in research, in collecting synonyms and occasionally in seeking out stylistic oddities?" Or again, the delight of philosophy: we have Marcus Aurelius' *Meditations*, we know his resolve to "clothe thyself in simplicity and modesty. . . . Only attend to thyself, and resolve to be a good man in every act. . . . Look within. . . . Retire into thyself"; for there only can be found the right measure for conduct, not in the pompous proportions of the emperor's actual rank. He shrinks from that, to be no more than a man. "Have a care lest you become a Caesar, lest you are dyed in purple," he admonishes himself.

3

Not much more than a hundred feet from this statue, not much more than a hundred years removed, is another statue, or a piece of one. It is the marble head of Constantine in the Palazzo dei Conservatori (plate II). It balances, bodiless, on a pedestal. From brow to chin, it measures six feet. Stains streak down its surface. The eyes that stare straight through the observer to some distant source of power, the great beak of a nose, the jaw protruding, all in superhuman size, astound and terrify.

Events that could persuade the Romans to turn from men to giants as rulers, that could so overwhelmingly remake the role of emperor into an embodiment of Herculean powers and authority, were events of no ordinary era. Its course began with the invasions which Marcus Aurelius faced on the northern frontier, and which he barely repulsed. Novelty lay not in the barbarian threat itself but in the fact that it could penetrate to Italy, and could reduce the emperor to the conscription of slaves into his army and the auctioning of the palace jewels and plate to fill up his war chest. The new era began, too, with the martyrs of Lyons—not that the harrying of Christians was new but that, for the first time under Marcus Aurelius, we have a full account of how a local persecution might arise. A few months earlier the throne had graciously decreed that victims for municipal arenas might be supplied henceforth by purchase of condemned criminals from officers of the state, at a trifling cost. Thus, when an explosion of anti-Christian hatred shook Lyons, the sufferers found themselves thrown to the beasts. One Christian, Attalus, was identified as a Roman citizen. His death was deferred, pending a decision from Marcus Aurelius on the legal implications of that status. The answer of the emperor in due time arrived. Roman citizens were only to be beheaded, and so they all were except Attalus himself, whom, "to please the people," the governor put to death by torture before an audience of many thousands.

A century's persecutions and invasions may stand for the invisible and visible forces that tore apart the empire, the former troubling men's minds, the latter threatening the amenities of a comfortable world: roads and streets and public baths, rural villas and suburban mansions, the rich man's summer flight to cooler country, the poor man's right to see bears baited and musical skits performed in the amphitheater. Not one of these things could be taken for granted any more. Instead, and in many regions for the first time in memory, men had physically to defend both life and property. Even in less vulnerable areas like Africa and Egypt, tribal chieftains launched their raids, even here brigands robbed travelers, people on journeys simply disappeared, and farms went up in smoke. Yet the real threat lay along the northern provinces. From Hadrian's Wall to the coasts of the Black Sea, a tide of war rolled in. Details of its progress for the most part escape us. What destroyed camps destroyed schools and libraries as well; what killed soldiers killed writers. In a society taken up with survival, little was left to sustain those literary circles that had earlier produced a Fronto. But some accounts remain, and archeologists can add the testimony of ashes marking the third-century strata of rural or urban sites. Coin hoards tell their story, too: hidden by fugitives and never claimed by their return, showing on the map of the Rhine and Danube provinces the successive limits of catastrophe just as the lines of flotsam on a beach show where high water reached. What was worst about the invasions, however, was not their coming in waves, again and again, but their coming together—their simultaneity in widely scattered places. For if the emperor could not be everywhere at once, then some local hero would volunteer to do his job, and by that act almost of necessity raised a rebellion requiring in its turn its own new forces, and new taxes to defend new claims, and new diversions of the empire's strengths to resist those claims. In the confusion, no one knew where his loyalty lay. Political stability once undermined, other consequences followed. Faith in the currency collapsed at a moment when everybody's expenses, especially the state's, were rising. Intercourse between cities and between provinces grew less safe and frequent at a moment when the need for everyone to pull together was most urgent. Life could be seen in some regions of the West reverting to the conditions that had obtained before the Roman conquest, before the introduction of general literacy or communications or currency, above all, before security. In the Rhone valley, people took to living in caves unoccupied since the Stone Age. In Britain and what is now Switzerland, hilltops that had been once the sites of villages solely on account of their defensibility were again built up. It was as if (in a most irregular pattern of distribution) the clock had been turned back a few generations here, or several centuries there, or a full millennium at some other point.

So much for the visible features of the crisis. The invisible were of the same order of gravity, and in many areas of thought similarly turned the clock back. From beneath the covering of a Greco-Roman homogeneity (never complete or perfect, of course) emerged the styles of art, the languages, the native worships that had prevailed before the legions came. It was a natural consequence of chaos. As men had to call on themselves for defense, so they did, to a different extent in different places, for the whole fabric of their life. Some degree of cultural separatism

matched political separatism. Among the things that suffered a change was religion. The Greco-Roman mixture
of the rational and the beautiful, which tested explanations
by reference to a highly developed aesthetic, or by reference to what could be known through sensory experience,
was in part forgotten, in part modified. Its answers had
proved too qualified, too complex, too slow in coming. In
its place, superstition. By any possible test we can make,
men born with Constantine were likely to hold ideas that
their predecessors, at the death of Marcus Aurelius, would
have rejected. From the later of the two periods we have
more lucky stones and amulets, more treatises on spells,
horoscopes, and enchantments, more charges of hexing
and laws against it, more mumbo jumbo in what passed
for philosophy, more appeal for aid from demons, more
miracles credited by the "more educated." All this will meet
us again when we come to consider Constantine's
conversion.

The invisible changes surveyed here were not welcomed
by contemporaries. Roman civilization was not in the
third century A.D. what it had been at the outset, the companion of conquering legions. It was not alien. Rather it
represented to the upper classes and probably also to the
mass of the population everywhere the normal condition of
things. It provided a setting for the good life, all the more
clearly in contrast with the agencies now challenging it. To
resurrect it in its former concord and serenity was the
dream that took hold of men's minds with increasing
power. Thus, working against innovation in beliefs and
manners was a marked cultural nostalgia, especially dominant in the leading ranks of society.

When order was restored, step by step over the reigns of
Claudius, Aurelian, and Diocletian (284–305), it bore the

stamp of conservatism. As so often after crisis—in the slogans of 1918, for example: return to normalcy, restoration and recovery—the key words of the later Empire began with that significant prefix, *re-*. The emperor was acclaimed the *restitutor, reformator, restaurator, reintegrator, redonator patriae, redditor lucis aeternae*. With the feeling expressed in these terms, Christianity collided head on. We must return to that conflict later. But the same feeling opposed itself to half-conscious revivals of local, submerged cultures. It could almost have been predicted that the successful champion of the state would therefore be a champion also of the state's oldest traditions. He would be required to draw together as much of the old ways as still made sense, to unify and synthesize and reconcile.

At the center of the old Roman tradition lay a pride in war, while at the center of the Roman failure in the third century lay its inadequacy in war. The heroes of the state in crisis were inevitably soldiers, often soldiers and nothing else, sometimes statesmen as well. No place for the flowing beard that marked a man of ideas, a philosopher, a Marcus Aurelius. That image was wrong for the times. Later emperors showed a smooth chin, or the stubble of a man in camp who simply has no leisure for shaving (so, Diocletian; plate IIA). No place, either, for the mild gaze of a ruler like Marcus Aurelius. Benevolence was softness, cultivation was effeminacy. Rome needed men of iron. Aurelian's nickname was Hand-on-Hilt; Diocletian ascended the throne by a most public murder of the one person who stood in his way. The type of face to which men responded was fixed in coin portraits, paintings, and marble busts for public distribution; so fixed, indeed, that over a period of two generations we are sometimes at a loss to tell one emperor from another, and they themselves could, without embarrassment, reuse each other's like-nesses simply by erasing the name. All shared the same thick neck, bullet head, bulging alert eyes, and prognathous jaw.

But it was not quite enough to be tough. The emperor must be great. Men demanded that much, if they under-stood the dimensions of the crisis. The majority who divined it less consciously or heard of its effects at second hand seem to have felt the same need. In the writings of this age we meet the former, that is, the conscious and analytical kind of observer, very rarely. Of a literature that was in any event in its decline, surviving fragments contain hardly a paragraph of comment on the underlying causes of the empire's troubles. Many of the symptoms, too, are passed over in silence. If contemporary sources have any fault to find, it is likely to be with the cowardice of the troops, the luxury and sloth of the emperor, or some sim-ilar, bookish, shallow focus of complaint. Only when we look beyond history proper are we rewarded with a deeper vision. It is as if people sensed more than they could express, as if demands of explanation had bankrupted the store of traditional ideas, and a substitute currency was required for the circulation of men's hopes and fears. The substitute was prophecy.

"A king of another race will arise in the West, master of a great force, godless, murdering, restless . . . , ruler of barbaric nations; and he will shed much blood. . . . In every city and in every place will be pillage and the raids of brigands and the shedding of blood." Again, in another text:

There arises a king toward the East with four peoples. He summons great numbers of tribes to himself in the city to bear aid, though he himself is the strongest. He crowds

the seas with thousands of ships, and whoever encounters
him is slain by the sword. . . . Hark to the hoarse sound from
the heavens resounding on all sides, terrifying the whole
earth as it falls in ruins. The sun flees pell-mell, the night
appears straightway on its heels, and God speaks out: How
long did you think I would be patient? His signal is given,
the plague rushes down from all the sky. The charge of fire
descends with thunderous noise, another and yet another
thunderbolt is hurled from the stars now, and the roars of
destructive slaughter are heard, the earth trembles, nor can
the whole human race make out where to turn.

Such were the predictions circulating in the second half of
the third century; such, too, the picture of horrific events
described in lines that Constantine quoted to an audience of
bishops in 323: "The very earth sweats," he recited; total
darkness will close in, mountains topple, rivers run dry, a
trumpet's voice will sound, and the Savior will appear.

What seems to speak through these revelations is the
knowledge shared among common people that they were
confronting a new dimension of danger, larger than past
experience, hence larger than could be grasped rationally.
Superhuman agencies were at work; strength to face them
could be found only in a savior of more than mortal size.
So into the old practices of emperor worship an added
longing was poured. His subjects magnified him because,
in the most literal sense of that word, they wanted to make
him bigger. The opposite resolve of Marcus Aurelius, to
"clothe himself in simplicity and modesty," belonged in the
past, along with the pretense that the emperor was a mere
five or six feet tall. Forty was better—just about the height
of the whole figure from which the head reposes in the
Palazzo dei Conservatori.

As a successor discovered, a generation after Constantine's death, an emperor who refused the role of colossus, who received his personal friends affectionately, addressed the citizens on terms approaching equality, dispensed with a great court retinue, and in other respects (including a beard) modeled himself on Marcus Aurelius, got nothing but criticism for his pains; whereas Constantine's son, and Constantine himself, we may be sure, aroused everybody's admiration by playing the giant—ducking his head slightly as he passed through the gates of Rome!

Entrance into a city, the *adventus*, offered men a rare glimpse of their ruler. In the world that Constantine was born into it had become a sort of act of state in itself. As the emperor approached, the senators, Roman or municipal, came out to meet him, accompanied by priests, magistrates, workers' guilds, constables, brass bands, and a crowd of lesser folk. He appeared borne on a litter or in a carriage; guards in gilt or silver armor flanked him, bearing silk banners designed to float inflated in the air, in the shape of dragons. The soldiers' shields were painted, the chariot painted and jeweled, the rider jeweled and robed in purple down to his shoes. Etiquette demanded that he make no response to the throng. He sat still and tried to look enormous. Political philosophers liked to find a resemblance to his own statue in his immobility, as in the metallic and inhuman stiffness of his knights; but for the common people, a resemblance lay closer to the images of gods enthroned in the temples.

By torchlight in the dark or over flower-strewn streets by daytime, the parade made its way, before Constantine, to the Capitolium, and after him, to his palace or a church, to the sound of rhythmic handclapping and unison shouts of good wishes, long life, thanks and supplication and salutes. Incense filled the air. That, and the torches and the four horses that drew his chariot, were his prerogatives alone, along with much else borrowed from the courts of Hellenistic kings, from the Roman triumph, from Persia, or from the accumulation of precedent. The whole was announced to the world by one of the chief instruments of propaganda, coins, bearing the legend ADVENTUS AUGUSTI or the like over a picture of the scene (plate IXв). No element was superfluous. An occasion so rich in staging and choreography, so floodlit, so advertised to everyone in its coming and completion, met some real need. Surely, that was the need to display to the people the one thing that bound together Africa and Gaul, tribesman and city-dweller: the emperor. Just as surely, it could no longer be Romanness, or the memory of some Republican hero, or even Jupiter to make a unity out of the empire.

A special house received the ruler in each of the cities he was most likely to visit, though preeminently in the place he chose as his capital. Palaces sprang up in Milan, Aquileia, Nicomedia, Antioch, and half-a-dozen other centers of the later third and earlier fourth centuries. They were marked, as we would expect, by size. A master who had to bow his head to fit under the gates of Rome required vast court-yards, vaulted corridors, and halls of state to live in, huge doors to enter; a gable above them, the sign of a god's residence; and on the floor (perhaps an innovation of Con-stantine's), in several locations where he was most likely to stand, a circle of porphyry, the purple stone, to receive his purple-shod foot. One inset circle of this kind would lie before the throne, itself porphyry and surmounted by an embroidered and glittering baldachin on four porphyry col-umns. Here would sit gigantic Rome embodied.

Few saw him, for few were admitted to his presence. Properly searched first for weapons, one passed through rows of guards and rows of ponderous pillars to some more specially solemn portal, opening to a hall fifty, a hundred, or two hundred feet long. At the far end, an apse screened off by a curtain; everywhere, silence. The visitor was escorted to the screen, spoke through it, and received his reply; or, if more privileged, had the curtain parted for him and advanced to the throne, first to kneel, then, still kneeling, to present a written petition held not in his contaminating hand but humbly covered in a fold of his garments. Certain ranks of officials were promoted through permission to kiss the emperor's robe, and might thereafter do so again whenever they were received in the palace. As we might predict, details of the reception, like details of the *adventus*, appeared on coins, in relief on various silver or ivory articles for distribution to notables, or in frescoes and mosaics. The portrayal is quite stereotyped because an occasion has become an institution, and the institution says to men: Here is your monarch, here is the gable above his head that sets off his divinity, here are his associates or sons, and to the sides stand his armored soldiers.

A third occasion, the *allocutio*. He addresses the army, himself in full military regalia, from a raised tribunal. They shout rhythmically, "Augustus Constantine! The gods preserve you for us! Your salvation is our salvation! In truth we speak, on oath we speak!" And this scene, too, is advertised on coins and in pictures (plate IXD), proclaiming in symbolic language the emperor's care for, and popularity among, the troops. Not many of them would be able to read, and an audience more remote—the men in distant camps—required a frequent reminder that they were the favored in the realm, that the emperor leaned on his soldiers and would reward them for their support. A gold piece in its value would carry that message plainly enough.

Allocutiones usually ended in imperial largesses. But the message was plainer still if it spoke through stamped reliefs. Art and actions, buildings and costumes and occasions, are used continually and emphatically as a means by which the emperor can speak to his subjects.

One almost imagines (wrongly; but one is meant to imagine) that the emperor never held a normal conversation with anybody. What he had to say was made known to his subjects in purple ink (if this is not a post-Constantinian development) and in an archaizing, florid chancery hand that challenged even experienced copyists. Sometimes they could not make it out at all. Style gave them equal difficulty. It was extremely conscious, the late descendant of centuries of rhetorical art, marked by many poetical tricks: avoidance of hiatus or of inelegant words; metrical terminations of sentences or clauses; variation through an apparently limitless vocabulary of periphrasis. The least note of anything politically embarrassing disappeared in Brahmsian harmonies; aimlessly rich orchestration obscured the theme, if any; inauspicious truths piped in vain against the drumrolls of hyperbole. And when he was addressed in turn, the emperor heard the same sort of language. Anything else would have been very bad manners, verging on *lèse majesté*. "One should not offer to the ears of so great a divinity anything that has not been long written and often recast. For whoever speaks extemporaneously before the emperor of the Roman people [here, Constantine] has no feeling for the greatness of the empire."

Besides style, content was prescribed by three hundred years of monarchy. With growing elaboration, the proprieties of praise had been worked out in generation after generation of Loyal Addresses to the throne. Not all were insincere. In the dark days of civil and foreign wars, still more in the days when some hope of better things seemed about to dawn, Romans discovered in their leaders a genuine greatness and in themselves a genuine gratitude. To use a terminology close to worship in describing everything imperial struck no one then as excessive. The Sacred Mint, or House, or Mind, or Decree, the Celestial this and Divine that, belonged by right and truth to the position of the emperor. So did panegyric. For instance: "Thou, our father, it befits to look down from the very summit of the empire to the common world and, with a sign of your heavenly head, to decree the fates of human affairs, to grant the auspices to those who prepare campaigns, to establish the laws that govern treaties of peace." Praise enough, perhaps; but it was a degree beyond this to be at a loss for words (as rhetors regularly alleged), to flounder in awe before such majesty. "No one has the right to judge princes, for in the very vestibule of their palaces the inquirer is driven back by a veneration that serves as a barrier, and whoever approaches their countenance nearer is bereft of sight, the rays cut off, as if his eyes were challenging the sun."

This artificial, elevated, and flattering form of speech infected communication in all but the lowest ranks of society. Consider only the beginning lines of a letter written by a monk in the 330's: "To the most genuine and most enlightened, most blessed, beloved and in God's keeping and filled with the Holy Ghost and most valued in the sight of the Lord God, Apa Paieou. . . ." Or consider the strict rules decreeing just who could and who could not kiss the robes, not of the emperor alone, but of certain of his officials. Ceremonies surrounding him appeared, with modifications determined by their distance from him, in every corner of the palace, and outside the palace in government or even private and domestic circles. One can imagine—indeed, one should never forget—the terribly heavy and unnatural atmosphere of court life.

One consequence was the isolation of the emperor. That, of course, was intended. It served to protect him, set against the history of many assassinations earlier in the third century. It served to raise him, too, above the common run of men. Among unfortunate consequences, however, it kept him from a true knowledge of much that he would have liked to find out about his own realm; worse, for us, it gave rise to a literature which in every department tolerated distortion of the truth. Historians must piece out a picture of the times from sources obviously and deliberately false, from panegyrics and eulogies, from the contorted elegance found even in legal documents, from euphemism, servility, bias, and a sort of affected distaste for the specific. Although these qualities are themselves an aspect of history, casting a characteristic light on the scene that we must observe and having an influence on the behavior of the actors, yet they have given rise to irremediable uncertainty about almost every point in Constantine's life. The reader, then, is warned.

II

IN THE EAST

Diocletian's realm included in both East and West wide areas of continuing or recent rebellion. The city of Rome for decades had ceased to serve as imperial headquarters. Thus the empire lacked clear boundaries and a clear center. The emperor, moreover, had no sons to help him in the tasks of recovery, and turned first to Maximian (titled Augustus or coregent in 286), next to two further associates in power on a somewhat lower level, the Caesars Galerius and Constantius (293). This arrangement, called the Tetrarchy, accommodated the divided condition of the empire and its scattered problems. While the senior Augustus made his capital near the Bosporus, at Nicomedia, he delegated a broad authority in the eastern regions to Galerius; Maximian from Aquileia at the head of the Adriatic delegated a broad authority in the eastern regions to Gale-Cooperation and subordination depended ultimately on personal loyalty and prestige; it was essential, and fortunate, that all four rulers worked well together. All sprang from similar undistinguished backgrounds in the lower Danube and Balkan regions, and had risen to the throne through government service, chiefly military. In these several respects they typified the careers which led to the top over the preceding half century, and which were again to supply successors to Constantine's dynasty when it terminated in his nephew Julian.

After a reign of twenty years, Diocletian resigned. His grip on things was loosening, his health and nervous strength were undermined; but for all that, abdication had no precedent. Still stranger was the decision to force Maximian also into retirement. These two steps, combined with the quasi-filial relation intended and for the most part realized between Augustuses and Caesars, suggested that the Tetrarchy in the mind of its creator was meant as a permanent constitutional innovation. There were always to be two senior and two junior emperors. The latter were to be chosen on a basis of merit, not descent, and were to succeed the former in their turn after some agreed term. Logical as it seemed, and despite its achievements, the Tetrarchy was nevertheless a highly artificial arrangement, an interim and merely lucky compromise. In the politics of Constantine's early life the central question thus was how soon the habit of hereditary monarchy would regain ascendancy. To this same question no less than six men offered six different answers. The years between 305 and 313 were chaotic, however, not only because in the nature of the Tetrarchy there had to be four holders of power, but because it was a period of transition leading back to an older system of rule. Since the death of Julius Caesar, the Roman empire had sought stability in the tradition that its head should bequeath his throne to his son; if he had no son, he adopted one. Even under the surface of Antonine "meritocracy," dynasticism retained its authority, and in the century that followed, up to Diocletian, emperors and pretenders alike promoted their own power by assiduously, sometimes absurdly, promoting their own offspring. Whether grown and able men or no more than little boys, these princes anticipated the challenge, Who, afterwards? and so established for the royal house a lien on the future. Merit, of course, always strengthened a claim, but that was an argument appealing more to panegyrists and philosophers. Among the masses of the empire what counted was rather the continuity of the imperial line. Dynasticism made sense; the Tetrarchy did not; and anyone with a feeling for the Roman way must have divined the history latent in the firstborn of the Caesar Constantius.

When the idea of hereditary monarchy later reemerged, a story was put about that Constantius' descent could be traced back to Claudius II (268-270). Whatever the truth of this, the Caesar who was appointed in 293 owed his promotion to his innate abilities, and amply displayed them in the suppression of independence and the firm reorganization of government in Gaul, the lower Rhine, and Britain. He proved to be a hard-hitting commander against the enemies of the state, mild to his subjects, and faithful to his fellow emperors. Even so, special measures were taken to insure his loyalty. He was obliged to divorce his wife Helena and marry Theodora, the daughter of Maximian; and Constantine, his son by Helena, was assigned a place, almost as a hostage, in the court of Diocletian. It is there that he first emerges into the light.

Of his earlier life nothing significant is recorded. Born at Naissus (Nis in eastern Jugoslavia) on February 17 of a year unknown, probably about 280, he saw little of his father. Helena could not be raised to a rank much above a barmaid by even the most enthusiastic of later traditions. Though she was to display piety and strength of character, and certainly attached her son to herself with an abiding love, she could not provide a background of cultivation. When he left home, he must have been an unlicked cub. It is said that his being sent to Diocletian's court was partly for the purpose of educating him, but there is more evidence of his physical growth than of his mental. He attained an average height but a very robust build and great strength. His fellows treated him with respect and nicknamed him Bullneck. He liked hunting, at least witnessed Diocletian's wars in Egypt in 295–296, and campaigned under the gross, rough, towering but soldierly Galerius against the Sarmatians a little later, giving a good account of himself in cavalry actions. He had, besides, won high rank in the troops of the Guard, and enjoyed more popularity with the army than quite pleased Galerius.

Galerius in the meanwhile had had his hands full with the eastern frontier. The Persians who invaded Syria in 296 had at first proved too much for him, and he required a second year to thrust them out and carry Roman victories into their homeland. At the moment, an attack of a different kind was making itself felt. The religion of the Persian prophet Mani had begun to penetrate the eastern provinces, exciting great fervor and destined for successes far-flung in time and space. Saint Augustine was for a while its convert, a century later, and it reemerged more than once in western Europe over the course of another thousand years. Given its origins among the most ancient of the empire's enemies, given, too, the conservatism of the Tetrarchy in religion especially, Manichaeism inevitably drew down the lightning of official wrath. It was pronounced a "superstitious doctrine of a most worthless and depraved kind," undermining the principles of all right-thinking Romans. "These principles," declared Diocletian, "it is not right to oppose or resist, nor ought the age-old religion be disparaged by a new one. For it is the height of criminality to re-examine doctrines once and for all settled by the ancients, doctrines which hold and possess their recognized place and course." The order to suppress

this infection, and to burn its scriptures, goes on to ex-
coriate its missionaries as disturbers of public tranquillity.

So they may well have been. That tranquillity, after all,
had been barely restored to a riven empire. It had not developed of itself, by a natural recovery, but by a violent
reorganization of life imposed from above. Public order
depended on constraint and rigor; its condition was still in
doubt; no troubling innovations could be permitted to dis-
tract men from the essential duty to close ranks. A military
metaphor was appropriate. Indeed, such were often to be
found in the emperor's edicts, with connotations of instant
compliance, of doing things "by the book," of uniformity
even in one's thoughts. Beyond that, rulers and subjects
shared the fears that found expression in prophetic literature, in visions of a universal Armageddon. Obedience and
conformity in conduct must then be matched in religion,
since only the gods could ward off new horrors. The belief speaks through official documents of the Tetrarchy.

For there can be no doubt that the immortal gods, as always
friendly to Rome, will be reconciled to us only if we have
provided that everyone within our realm pursues a pious
and religious peace and a life thoroughly pure in all re-
gards. . . . For our laws safeguard nothing but what is holy
and venerable, and it is in this way that the majesty of Rome,
by the favor of all the divine powers, has attained such
greatness.

The two levels of Rome's guardians, human and divine, the
two levels of treason that may be shown against the state
and against its official and historic cults, are joined in
thought again and again, in this and the next generation.

If Rome's good fortune rested on the gods, then they

might surely withhold it from a people that denied them
their due. Christians aroused hatred precisely for this reason, that they would not join their fellow citizens in necessary acts of worship. They were, according to the most
common charge, atheists, strange as it sounds to us; and to
their refusal of worship, jeopardizing the *pax deorum*, they
added an express determination to convert everyone sooner
or later to their own dangerous views. Certainly there had
been other charges also in the first and second centuries, but
these arose from ignorance as much as anything else, and in
the third century few people credited the old stories of in-
cest and cannibalism; they persisted only in the belief that
intransigent impiety might alienate the gods. For illustration, take two incidents leading up to the last agony of the
Church. In the first, while Diocletian was sacrificing in
public, the chief interpreter of the victim's organs reported
that he could not read the future in them because of the
hostile influence of Christians standing around. Diocletian
burst into a rage, insisted that all in his court should offer
sacrifice, and sent out orders to his army to follow suit.
Though no general persecution developed, Galerius' agents
were encouraged in individual acts against Christians, some
of whom were dismissed from the army, some executed,
while their enemy in private continued to press his older
colleague in the same direction as his own. At last, in the
second incident, an inquiry about the Christians was sent to
Delphi, and Apollo answered that if his oracle had fallen
silent or no longer predicted as infallibly as of old, they
were the ones to blame. The notion of hexing, if the word is
not too small for a threat to the whole Roman world, governs both incidents.

The Great Persecution which now began (303–312) belongs to history as a whole rather than to the career of

Constantine in particular. If he played any part in it, which is unlikely, at any rate no account survives. To explain events in which he did take a part later, however, attention should be drawn to one point: the degree of popular tolerance of Christianity as opposed to the extraordinarily cruel and widespread official pressure bearing down on it. In fact, the two often seem at odds, throwing light on the way in which events, looked at through the eye of prescience, were likely to develop. The ultimate triumph of a narrow paganism was surely improbable if Diocletian's own wife and daughter had deserted it, or were at least under suspicion of having done so; if his minister of finance had espoused Christianity, and died for it; if other martyrs included officials of the palace staff as well as its lower servants; if the army produced its share, too, in what numbers we cannot very well estimate, but in widely scattered units; and if distinguished private citizens professed their faith also, from the noble who tore down the first posted edict (St. George, in some accounts) to the municipal senators selected for a more humane death. Naturally Christian tradition emphasized its heroes of a higher station. Eusebius, Lactantius, and other writers were not immune to the prevalent sense of rank, and took pride in converts from among the educated and prominent classes. But Christianity had really advanced a long step toward the center of the stage, especially during the previous half century. Only a sprinkling in the West, and wholly lacking in the rural areas, its adherents in the eastern and African provinces made up some large percentage of the population, in a few areas a majority, concentrated in those points of greatest economic and political importance, the towns and cities, and adequately organized to administer ecclesiastical funds, lands, and buildings. Clandestine communities were a thing of the past. In Nicomedia, the church stood near the palace itself, and Diocletian and Galerius, on February 22, 303, the day before the first edict, posted themselves by a window watching their soldiers engaged in its pillage and debating whether to destroy it by fire. They decided not to, lest the fire spread to the palace.

The screws of oppression tightened over a period of years, loosened, and tightened once more. Each year bore its own degree of suffering. Moreover, marked differences emerged in the policies of both higher and lower officials. In the West, Constantius acted with restraint, up to his death in 306, and Maximian seems to have ignored the later, crueler edicts in Africa. In the East a true, hot fanaticism governed Galerius and, after 305, Maximin Daia; yet they had trouble in generating the same fervor among the masses. So long as institutions acted on institutions, all went smoothly. Persecution was initiated in the highest government circles, its legists drafted decrees, its soldiers nailed them up in public places and enforced them on the community, confiscating, destroying, or locking up buildings, scriptures, and articles of silver used in divine service; proceeded next to decapitate the congregation, so to speak—a merciful death—by the arrest of its officials, its bishops, deacons, exorcists, and so forth; and in general seem to have made use of established instruments of law and order. We see the governors obeying their superiors' instructions. Municipal authorities are geared into the process. Local constables are posted at the city gates to interrogate people methodically as they pass in and out—"Are you a Christian?"—or work their way through tax lists, the ancient equivalent of telephone directories, to tick off the names of persons seized or acquitted, one by one. The same unprecedented powers that had hauled the empire back from the brink of collapse, a decade or two before, were now directed to the annihilation of a final danger.

But the danger would not yield; therefore severer measures. Revolts were promptly put down in Syria and Melitene.

In Phrygia, soldiers surrounded a small town of Christians, every single citizen there, and setting fire to it burnt it down along with the women and children as they called on the God of all; for all those who inhabited the town without exception, the curator himself and the magistrates and everyone else in office and the whole people, professed themselves Christians.

The account is Eusebius', who knew what he was talking about. Elsewhere, wrote one who witnessed what he described, and shortly died a martyr,

as the soldiers competed in their acts with each other, [the Christians] held fast to their resolution; for perfect love casteth out fear. What account would suffice to list the acts of bravery and manliness in every test? For permission being granted to anyone who wished to assault them, some beat them with sticks, others, with rods or whips or thongs or ropes, presenting a changing spectacle of torture filled with wickedness. Some had their hands tied behind them and were hung up on the gibbet, racked in every limb by mechanical devices. Then the torturers on orders worked over their whole bodies with their instruments of punishment, not as they do to homicides, on the flanks only, but on the belly, legs, and cheeks. Others were hung up from the porch by one hand, suffering the worst of agonies from the stretching of their limbs and joints.

Eyes and tongues were cut out, feet lopped off; many endured a red-hot iron chair, or molten lead, death at the stake, wild beasts in the amphitheater, drowning, starvation, hanging, decapitation, or a slower release through months or years of imprisonment in packed and fetid dungeons. From the horrifying pages of Eusebius or Lactantius the reader would protect himself by imagining that their descriptions were "much exaggerated." Distrust of later inflated legends, even a smile at the quaintness of Foxe's *Book of Martyrs*, may lead scholars to wonder if the Great Persecution was "really all that bad." It was.

But two factors prevented it from anticipating the twentieth century. The bureaucracy was by comparison crude and ineffective, and the emperors experienced considerable difficulty in raising the general populace to the desired pitch of ferocity. Christians were men's neighbors, or relatives. One bought one's wine or onions from them and saw them in the public baths revealed down to their very nakedness as human beings not worse but probably better than oneself. For all the roughness of life, taking into account also the indifference that came from the witnessing of ordinary public executions or gladiatorial combats, it was not easy in those times to communicate the government's purpose to the man in the street. His patience of cruelty, in however worthy a cause, began to give out. His zeal, even if he sympathized with official policy, flagged. Maximin Daia, emperor in the East from 305 to 313, toward the end of his reign was obliged in a general edict to solicit from the cities of his realm requests for the preservation of the old rites, by which men were assured of "crops heavy with ears of corn flourishing in the broad plains, meadows through good rains radiant with plants and flowers, the weather granted us temperate and mild . . . the calmest peace en-

joyed securely and quietly," etc., etc., etc. Such requests
were to be linked to the inviting in of imperial aid against
the enemies of the present bountiful *pax deorum*. "That
you may know," continues Maximin Daia, "how welcome
your resolution on this matter has been to us, and how
willingly zealous and benevolent our spirit is, quite apart
from your decrees and petitions, we grant to your piety to
ask whatever benefaction you wish as the reward of your
godly purposes." In short, he would pay for cooperation.
Antioch, for one, took advantage of the offer. It had been
advertising its pagan altars on its coinage for some years,
and now a prominent trimmer arose to direct the hunting
up of Christians and their expulsion beyond the city walls.
The Assembly of Lycia followed suit with an official letter
to the emperors.

Since your kinsmen the gods have ever shown their love
of mankind to all, O most renowned monarchs, by whom
their worship has been zealously fostered and who pray to
them for the eternal salvation of yourselves, our all-con-
quering lords, it has seemed right to us to hasten to your
immortal sovereignty to request that Christians, long a source
of civil division and ever defending that plague [their religion]
up to the present moment, should desist, and should violate
the honor due to the gods with no ill-omened innovations,
as would best be accomplished if it should be established
by your divine and eternal command that the hated worship
of these atheists in all its wickedness should be renounced and
prevented, and that they be required to devote themselves
continually to the cult of the gods, your kinsmen, on behalf
of your eternal and indestructible rule, as is clearly to the
advantage of all your subjects.

The petition reflects the style of address befitting official
communication with the majesty of the throne. Its rather

flaccid prose reflects, too, the attitude of paganism toward Christianity by 311, after eight years of intermittent disorder, frightening sights and sounds, and the harrying of the innocent. During the persecution's later stages in all areas, and throughout its course in some areas, its agents showed a tendency to draw back from the extremity of harshness. That fact resulted in curious scenes.

We find, to our surprise, that Egyptian confessors who had been transferred to the mines of southern Palestine were there able to put up makeshift buildings for worship and to conduct services all but openly. At Alexandria likewise the prisoners, including the bishop, Peter, of that city, and Meletius, bishop of Lycopolis, were left very much to themselves. Like somewhat similar groups over the last century, confined literally or figuratively underground, crowded and cramped, and passing through days of utter stagnation into days of acute danger, these Christians split apart. The natural point of dispute was the treatment of their brothers who, in one degree or another, had betrayed Christ to the persecutors. Peter advocated leniency, Meletius, severer measures. A curtain was rigged up in the enormous room that held them, to divide the two camps; and in their vicissitudes thereafter, that is, from 306 onwards till peace returned, each struggled to place its own adherents in posts left vacant by renewed arrests. In the mines of Palestine the schismatics established their Church of the Martyrs among the convicts, challenging the Catholics; in Egypt, where the schism had begun and took root, men who were at the moment in prison nevertheless received or made appointments as bishops and presbyters. After their release into the sunlight of toleration, they continued their intrigues. Meletianism penetrated the structure of the Church throughout the province within a decade.

Rigorist views were a common aftermath of persecution. They had proved so in the 250's, for example, in Rome and Africa, and now appeared there again. While the disputes in the capital, however, produced no permanent results, in Carthage events took a different turn. Donatism was born, grew to strength, and plagued Constantine's reign. We will return to that story in due course.

In the meantime, the chief enemies of Christianity had departed from the scene, in circumstances affording a cruel joy to Lactantius. His account of *The Deaths of the Persecutors* looks for proof that God destroys those who destroy His servants. History obliged. In 304, on his way back from Rome to Nicomedia, Diocletian fell sick. His condition held him to his bed throughout the winter, rumors that he had finally succumbed circulated daily in the palace, and when, in March of 305, to everyone's surprise he again made his appearance in public, he looked like death. Sixty may have been no great age. On the other hand, he had lived hard. He had suffered spells of insanity or incoherence at the height of his illness, and wept easily. Pressed by Galerius, he decided on abdication. The stage was set for the formal transfer of power on May 1, 305, a few miles outside Nicomedia at a place marked by a column dedicated to Jove. Ringed by picked regiments and surrounded on the platform by the chief members of his court, Diocletian tearfully announced the ebbing of his vigor and the need he felt to end his reign. Galerius and Constantius were to become Augustuses. A new pair of Caesars were presented to the army, Flavius Valerius Severus and Maximin Daia, Galerius' nephew.

Though there was no difficulty about their promotion, these two were little known, and doubtless Lactantius is right in saying that the troops had entertained different expectations. Maximian's son Maxentius was there, of an age suited to the job and shortly to prove that he could grasp it unaided. If he had been chosen, however, he would have enjoyed much power of his own, given the popularity of his father among the soldiers and their habit of thinking in dynastic terms. Similar reasons weighed against Constantine. He would not, like Severus or Maximin Daia, have been Galerius' creature, and he might well have received the backing of Maximian from behind the scenes. As early as 293 an engagement had apparently been arranged between Maximian's daughter Fausta, and Constantine, though their marriage did not take place until 307. Whatever Galerius' calculations, however, one thing was clear: He meant to be master.

A message soon arrived from Constantius, pleading ill health and asking that his son be released to him. Galerius delayed, thinking no kind thoughts of the young hostage. Legends describe the plots against Constantine's life, through convenient boars or barbarians, hunts or wars. At last Galerius consented to his leaving; the *congé* was official. Taking no chances of the emperor's change of mind, Constantine anticipated a more ceremonious departure by a wild nighttime flight, in his bolt for freedom killing the post-horses behind him and no doubt half killing those he rode himself. When Galerius woke up next day, the bird had flown, and pursuit was impossible.

III

IN THE WEST

Constantine was not to see Nicomedia again for nearly twenty years, until 324. The region he now entered was deeply different from the one he had left, with differences the more striking to him because of the speed of his passage. Climate aside—and Nicomedia cannot ordinarily be mistaken for London—the East spoke Greek and displayed its culture in its cities as if in jewel boxes, while the West spoke Latin and spread its far poorer treasure over towns and villas; the East was old and safe, the West young and armed.

At the time that Constantius became Caesar his chief work was to cleanse away the chaos of alien invasions. Another agent of the imperial recovery, Carausius, was himself sprung from the Menapii (in what is now Belgium) and, entrusted in 288 with large naval forces, promptly revolted, drawing in to his command sufficient recruits from the half-tamed tribes of the lower Rhine to control the Channel, gain Britain, man a fleet, and guard his headquarters at Boulogne. His empire did incorporate a whole Roman substructure of soldiers, officials, and civilians, but the most active part in it was played by tribesmen from the Low Countries, chiefly the Franks attracted by hope of pillage. Driven from Boulogne, and their leader Carausius replaced by another of their number, the barbarians were not finally subdued to their proper role until 296, when Constantius' coins advertised his triumphant entrance into London, under the heading, Restorer of Eternal Light.

It was in fact a somewhat dim light; and the nearest thing to eternal about it was the barbarian element now entering on the long, long period of its ascendancy. There were no Roman legions adequate to hold down the region of the lower Rhine. Not Latin-speaking men but the Salii were settled as farmers and guardians of these half-submerged lands, while other surrounding branches of the Frankish people were permitted to remain under their own chieftain Gennobaudes. Franks had been admitted to ravaged areas around Trèves at the start of Constantius' reign, as his son was there to add further groups of Sarmatae; it was Constantius, again, who in the words of a rhetor of 297 handed over to "the plow of the barbarians all the deserted territories around Amiens, Beauvais, Troyes, and Langres"; yet it was at Langres that a sudden raid of Alemanni caught Constantius so by surprise that he had to run for his life, and, since the panicky folk inside had slammed shut the city gates, he had to be hoisted to safety by ropes let down to him over the walls. In truth, barbarian penetration proved quite impossible to control. Men might be subdued, they might be let in to the empire on terms permitting the conqueror to levy taxes on their farms and recruits from among their children. But even if they kept the open part of their bargain, they insensibly and involuntarily undermined the edifice they were supposed to support. The empire, after all, was more than a thing of bricks and mortar, more than camps or frontier barriers. It was a civilization, worth fighting for only so long as the boundaries of culture defined it, and defined its enemies. In those towns today called Francs, Sermaise (from Sarmatae), or Marmagne (from Marcommanni) an alien life took root, destined to assert its influence in widening circles against the weakening differentness of Roman Gaul. When Constantine saw these regions first he could not fail to notice the jewelry, brooches, glassware, and pottery characteristic of the Alemanni around Basel. As he traveled on, similar traces, in a range of objects beyond archeological recovery, would have betrayed to him the presence of various foreign tribes at Cologne, Rheims, and elsewhere. Their graves today explain why they were welcomed inside the frontier: they were great warriors. Thus they were buried with a wholly un-Roman assortment of axes, knives, swords, arrows, and spears, richer for their chiefs and nobles, poorer for mere followers, but in either case bearing a Germanic stamp.

Constantius nevertheless made use of these tribes as necessity dictated. His subjects applauded. Only in scale did the practice go beyond precedent, and, then as now, no one could read the future. He rebuilt castles and towers all along the Rhine, and behind this screen the orchards and vineyards once more grew up, fields long abandoned were cleared, farmhouses and villas rose again in the river valleys. At Autun, standing for the cities of his realm in general, his troops went to work patching the aqueduct; he imported artisans from Britain to restore temples and basilicas; and to the local schools he gave his own secretary-in-chief as professor, suitably endowed in every sense. The grateful recipient testified, perhaps with some exaggeration, to the donor's "great facility in public speaking of every sort," while modestly depreciating his own. He sees the emperor "pursuing literature with a zeal so great as to consider the art of eloquence no less suited to his divine providence than the art of beneficence." He expands on the latter, and the emperor's popularity. A pleasant story lends support. Constantius preferred to leave the wealth of his provinces diffused among the people rather than locked away in government coffers; he failed, that is, as his fellow Tetrarchs saw it, to collect taxes strictly enough. Diocletian thought to bring home to him the consequences of such kindness, but Constantius simply called together a number of his richest subjects and explained the fix he was in. Diocletian's messenger was thunderstruck to see them, on the instant, offer vast sums of gold voluntarily, which Constantius later privately returned to them.

Christians had special reason to be pleased with the condition of Gaul. If a few of them perhaps suffered martyrdom (that question is open) it was through local initiative, not as a result of any official persecution by Constantius himself; if churches were destroyed, as Lactantius says, it was at least on a scale that Eusebius could later deny altogether. If the emperor was no Christian, one could at any rate refer vaguely to his acknowledging of the Supreme Being; and among his relations, besides the converts Constantine and Helena, one son later married a Christian, and a daughter received at some time the Christian name Anastasia, possibly only on baptism. Constantius' morals were unexceptionable; and with seven children one could fairly call him a family man. All things considered, the Church must have welcomed his successor from within his own line.

He succumbed to his illness in the palace at York on July 25, 306, the first of the Tetrarchy to die, the first to be declared a god after his death. Constantine had reached him only a month or two earlier, in sufficient time, however, to take part in a successful campaign to the north and to make himself known and respected by the soldiers. They saw in him a physical resemblance to his father, a handsome high color, short, somewhat wavy hair, firm jaw, broad shoulders, manly bearing—and a willingness to pay for his election. Moreover, they responded instinctively to the claims of descent. On his first appearance before the house troops, and specially favored by the powerful Alemannic chieftain Crocus, he was hailed as emperor. Donatives stimulated universal rejoicing. From that day he dated his reign.

These happenings aroused different responses in the several quarters to which they were reported. At Trèves, though the mints had to bestir themselves, they were at the sad disadvantage of not knowing what their new master looked like; so the face on the coins offered up only the clichés of contemporary imperial portraiture. It was a symbolic instance of how the role might overwhelm the individuality of the actor (plates IID & E). At Serdica (modern Sofia) Galerius received the laurel-wreathed portrait of Constantine, the paint no doubt still wet, in ritual announcement of the steps that had been taken at York. The ritual answer was either to burn it, or send back a purple robe. Galerius was obliged to choose the latter gesture, modifying its significance, however, by accepting Constantine only as his subordinate Caesar, at the same time raising Severus from Caesar to Augustus in Constantius' place. At Rome, Maxentius looked at Constantine's portraits with rage and jealousy. Who was this other to be emperor, while he himself was nothing? Largesses to the praetorian guard, a few murders, and the job was done. Maxentius heard himself acclaimed as emperor on October 28, and, after some experiments in titulature, late in 306 stood forth as Augustus.

Finally, enemies beyond Rome's frontiers learned of the changes on the throne and saw in them a chance for attack. We hear very confusedly of the Franks crossing the lower Rhine; of their two chiefs captured and killed in Trèves' amphitheater; of further Roman revenge exacted along the coasts of the Low Countries; of Roman armies thrust forward against the Bructeri north of the Ruhr; and of victories gained over the Alemanni to the east. In October the latter gave occasion to triumphal games, advertised on the victor's coinage. This time the mints knew their man. Constantine was assuming the necessary lines and proportions of a great soldier.

People in Gaul, not ignorant of Vergil, might recall the verses, "To spare the conquered and war down the proud." But when they contemplated the atrocities inflicted by their armies on the foe—methodical mayhem, cattle butchered or led away, villages burned, and thousands of captives claimed for the amphitheater, the army, or slavery—their thoughts took a different turn. "It is a stupid clemency that spares the conquered foe," in the words of Constantine's panegyrist. The same response meets us on coins. The emperor is pictured under the legend Gloria Constantini Augusti (plate IXc), dragging a captive by the hair, kicking another, or cleverly doing both together, or galloping across barbarian bodies; the phrase "Romans' rejoicing" boastfully surmounts weeping or suppliant personifications of "The Alemanni conquered." In 307/8, the construction of a bridge at Cologne, which served as entrant into hostile country and produced, in itself alone, copious surrenders, delighted Constantine's subjects. They exulted again over his crushing of the Alemanni and Franks in 310, and the Franks once more in 313. Beyond all precedent, harsh as Rome had always been, the gulf between We and They deepened, the ruler and his armies rose higher above a hapless enemy, all cruelties were excused, all "barbarians" lumped together. In coins and relief sculpture alike, a new lack of fellow feeling for the conquered makes its appearance under Constantine, continuing under his successors. Yet at the same time, as we have seen, Rome depended more than ever before on barbarians to defend her borders, not simply in an auxiliary status like that of Julius Caesar's Gallic cavalry, so long ago, but as the select core of the imperial bodyguard, in growing numbers, and from that, by "seconding" and promotion, to other still higher ranks. What rulers of the third century had begun, Constantine developed further. That *Debellator gentium barbarorum* in his crucial campaign of 312 took with him strong contingents of various Gallic and Germanic tribes (according to one source, his entire expeditionary army), two casualties of which seem to be recorded on gravestones in Italy, both belonging to units from Deutz, both officers. On his triumphal arch in Rome we can see such warriors in his entourage, their shields decorated in a characteristic Celtic fashion with opposed animal heads—specifically, goats' heads, suggesting the crack troops called Cornuti, suggesting also the totemism endemic in Celtic worship. Other similar units are known, of like heraldry: the Angelevarii, the Brachiati. And once more, too, in the battles that brought him sole rule in the empire (324), Constantine relied on barbarian troops. In this war they were Goths.

A Gothic chieftain who came to Constantine at his new capital rejoiced to see a statue of himself put up in the very senate house, an honor which we may guess was paid to him as a defender of the Danubian frontier; and Eusebius recalls how

we ourselves sometimes happening to be at the gates of the palace have seen lines of barbarians of remarkable aspect standing there, with distinctive costumes and with different types of appearance, hair, and beards, grim faces, terrifying glance, and surpassing bodily size; some with red complexions, some pale as snow, some blacker than ebony or pitch, some of a coloring in between. . . . Each in turn, as in a painting, brought to the emperor what was of value to each, some bearing gold crowns or diadems set with precious gems, or blonde children [as slaves], or clothing embroidered in gold and flowers, or horses, shields, long spears, bows and arrows, showing that they offered by these means their service and alliance to the emperor, if he would accept them.

Strange as these visitors may have seemed, they were hardly more so than the towering men who stood on duty at the palace doors, lined the corridors, and admitted to the imperial presence; no stranger than Crocus, who served so prominently with Constantius and who helped to secure the accession of his son, or Bonitus the Frank who held command against Licinius, or the Germanic duke of the province Second Pannonia, Aurelius Januarius. Constantine's nephew accused the emperor of opening even the consulate to barbarians. This we may doubt; yet within half a century of Constantine's death these very processes had gone far to change the Roman into the medieval world.

The only route by which barbarians could reach the palace in the fourth century (and the throne, in the fifth) lay through military service. Thus the background to their prominence under Constantine is the reorganization of the Tetrarchic and Constantinian army.

Broadly speaking, the army of Marcus Aurelius consisted in equal parts of legions and auxilia, the latter second class in pay, training, citizen status, and prospects for advancement. Both types of troops were stationed near points of danger in camps that had grown more and more permanent. Emergencies had to be met by temporarily robbing one area of its strength to reinforce some other; and the system, governed ultimately by considerations of economy, thus proved unable to cope with major threats on two or more fronts at once. Over the third century, an obvious step was taken: The army was enlarged. A second step was the creation of a mobile reserve on a far grander scale than the praetorian guard. Its core was naturally mounted, and, almost as naturally, barbarian, since the typical peasant of the provinces was good material only for the infantry. The resulting split within the armed services developed steadily. On the frontier (the *limes*), immobile and less valued *limitanei* included tribesmen such as have been mentioned, brought into the empire on terms obliging them sometimes to defend their territory, sometimes to contribute their sons to local army units. Militia of a mixed function, agricultural and military, held down certain other stretches of country, for example, in north Africa, lodged in fortified farm-houses. Even the more regular frontier army corps now guarded not the great five- or fifty-acre stone camps of the Empire at its height, but mean fortlets strung along the Rhine and Danube, perched on sub-Alpine hilltops, or clustered in depth at the edge of the Syrian desert. A spirit of stagnation, of demoralized make-do, settled gradually over the *limitanei*.

The mobile *comitatenses*, on the other hand, enjoyed an enviable prestige. That, and their name, derived from their nearness to the center of bounty and power, the emperor. They were his Companions. Under the Tetrarchs they had been few, and the glitter they might otherwise have claimed attached still to the praetorian guard in Rome. With the disbanding of the latter by Constantine in 312, the *comitatenses* quickly emerged as an institution, comprising the best part, and a large one (at least a quarter), of the whole empire's armed strength. Despite their name, we cannot

imagine that so numerous a category all had their barracks
in the capital, but they were concentrated in much fewer
and much larger groups than the *limitanei*, and those who
were stationed behind one or another length of frontier
would accompany the emperor when he assumed personal
command, providing maneuverability and striking power.
A criticism made of Constantine by a fifth-century writer,
that he had built up this force at the expense of the border
troops, of course contained some truth; Constantine went
beyond all previous emperors in withdrawing the best blood
to the *comitatenses*, weakening especially the border cavalry; and we may add that the impetus for his policy probably arose out of private ambition. The most likely
consideration that guided the steps he took was not the
relatively mild threat from tribes beyond the Rhine and
Danube, but the need for an expeditionary army in his civil
wars, notably in 312 and 324. For all that, we know he also
raised entirely new regiments which we can identify by
their names, Constantiniani or the like. More important,
what he did worked. Whether because of subsidies to client
states, or the control of hostile pressure by admitting barbarians into the empire, there to defend it as their own;
whether because of movements of peoples to the north that
we know nothing about, or because of the balance of weapons embodied in the mixture of *limitanei* and *comitatenses*—for whatever reason, the invasions of the third
century were not repeated on anything like an equal scale
in the fourth. The direction of development indicated by
Constantine was followed out by his successors.

The same circumstances controlling his military policy
led to the formation of two smaller élites, the *protectores*
and the *scholae*. The former grew up within the *comitatenses* as the emperor's bodyguard. A handful under Diocle-

tian, they numbered some thousands in the latter part of Constantine's reign. Into their ranks were enlisted the pick of the military, the young and noble, or men distinguished at a riper age by their service in other units. They were the lowest of those allowed to adore the sacred purple, that is, to kiss the imperial cloak. Resident for a few years in the court, they enjoyed the chance to make their merits known to the chiefs of staff. They rapidly became an officer school, going off to distant commands; and, predictably as their numbers grew, late under Constantine or not long after his death, they had subdivided further into their rank ordinary, serving the palace generally, and *protectores domestici,* who attended personally on the emperor.

All of the troops so far described obeyed a new pair of commanders (beginning in the early 320's): the Master of Cavalry and the Master of Infantry. To the praetorian prefects, of their former military responsibility, all that remained was the oversight of pay and provisioning. The prefects might receive an honor guard, but it was now drawn from the *protectores;* in place of the once-decisive praetorian cohorts were the *scholae palatinae,* wholly cavalry, the innermost ring of steel around the throne, taking their name from the hall near the palace entrance where they lodged. Their total, perhaps twenty-five hundred at first, was increased in later reigns. When we hear of the resplendent figures in full mail, on jeweled steeds, gilt and gleaming at every point of their equipment, who flanked the imperial carriage or guarded the gates of the imperial residence, it is these special Scholarians who are meant. And on the principle governing so many areas of Constantine's military policy, indeed of military policy throughout the later Roman Empire, these men who stood nearest him were not only barbarians, almost without exception, but

Franks from clear beyond the frontier. The more barbarian, the more valued. That was the rule. As one moved upward through the ranks, and inward from the periphery to the center of the empire, the presence of barbarians became more pronounced. Though the Scholarians acquired Roman names and learned Latin, nevertheless Constantine saw among those physically closest to him men who were farthest from him in culture.

Another new post originated under Constantine (before 320): the Master of Offices. He commanded the *scholae palatinae*. He also commanded an equally prominent, even notorious, corps now first recruited to serve him, the Agents of Affairs. Their title recalls other officials of our own century, under a bland exterior performing most unpleasant duties for Central Security, or Intelligence, for the State Political Administration, the Extraordinary Commission, and so forth. The Agents of Affairs were, in fact, secret police. As to the "Offices" controlled by the Master, chief among them were "Admissions," "Petitions" (so one may translate *memoriae*), "Diplomatic Correspondence" (*epistulae*), and "Appeals" (*libelli*).

Before turning to the last broad area of his administration, we should note what was common to this as well as to the pair of army Masters mentioned above. All three borrowed their authority from the praetorian prefecture. That cluster of jurisdictions, chief recipient of whatever military or civil powers overflowed from the emperor, had served as springboard for a dozen plots and revolutions during the course of the Empire. In untrustworthy hands, it became progressively more dangerous as government became more centralized. Even the loyalest servant found it almost impossible to administer competently. Under the Tetrarchs there had been two (less likely, four) praetorian prefects, and under them their fourteen representatives, *vicarii*, to supervise fourteen groups of provinces. That arrangement did something to solve the problem of excessive centralization. But when the number of prefects, step by step with the emperors, was reduced to two (with Licinius and Constantine) by 313, and to one by 324, and when the business of government continued simultaneously to increase, some better system had to be devised. Constantine decided to retain the *vicarii;* for a time he retained the old praetorian prefecture, too. In 317, however, he assigned to his son Crispus the rule of Gaul with a praetorian prefect to assist him. A similar procedure was followed later with another son. This casual multiplication of prefectures suggested the best way to absorb the problems of Licinius' realm after 324, by making an institution out of an experiment. The result was the so-called regional prefecture—rather, four of them, extending (very roughly) over the East, the Balkans, Italy plus Africa, and Gaul plus Britain. At the same time, as we have seen, many praetorian responsibilities were shifted to new officials, notably the three in charge of Cavalry, Infantry, and Offices. The history of these particular changes must be completed in a later chapter, but may serve at this point to illustrate the operation of a chain of cause and effect that can be seen at work everywhere in the period: from problems to solutions and then to an expanded government to administer those solutions. Contemporaries occasionally protested against the rising number of officeholders, but it is difficult to see where the chain of developments could have been properly and usefully broken.

Returning to the final duty of the Master of Offices: He had to see that the court moved from place to place comfortably, and that in the capital or wherever else it might settle, its members all found accommodations. That was no small job. The emperor was the government, in theory; various bureaus were attached to him, not to any set of rooms or buildings; and he never seemed to stay put. Doubtless on campaigns he left much business to be transacted in his absence; on the other hand, in the more or less typical stretch of fourteen months (March, 316, to June, 317) we find him issuing laws from temporary headquarters at Chalons, Vienne (on the Rhone), Arles, Verona, Serdica (Sofia), and Sirmium (on the Save). Earlier in his reign his movements are little known, and in the half-dozen years before his death he traveled much less. Still, we must not picture him ordinarily fixed and sedentary at the center of his realm. Rather, in the fashion of most of his predecessors over the span of a century, he had many centers, of which Rome for a while, thereafter Constantinople, was only the most official.

With him were present (again, in theory) certain chiefs of his government responsible directly to himself, for no large clusters of subordinate power were to be permitted—the Masters, two Counts handling treasury matters, a legist, a chamberlain, and others—who with their assistants may be reckoned up to at least five hundred. If many were away for one reason or another, the total of those who did accompany the court on any journey, or at any place of sojourn, must be multiplied to take into account their personal servants. We happen to know the style in which one of Constantine's lower officials traveled, taking along a personal trumpeter and a numerous household staff. Behind him came his baggage: six tunics, six heavy shirts, two light cloaks, one heavy, three wraps, one turban, towels, assorted sandals and leggings, jewelry, linen, bedding, tapestries, lamps, cups, spices, foods, and wines. Would the people and their belongings fit in (let us say) three carriages, or on the backs of a mere dozen horses? Would the whole imperial retinue make up a procession only (let us say) three miles in length? But we may leave that nightmare to the Master of Offices.

Constantine, like his father, made his headquarters at Trèves (Trier) on the Moselle. It recommended itself by its nearness to the frontier, where his chief business usually lay; besides, in 306 it had already seen more than a decade of use as a government center, with all that that meant in terms of expanded facilities. Here was an established mint, feeding its issues to all the armies of the Rhine. Here, too, was a provincial governor; a Duke of the *limes;* imperial factories for the production of uniforms, court dress, shields, and spears; the treasury for Gaul, including a bureau in charge of crown properties and another for the collection of taxes; and, we may add, after 318 a praetorian prefect and his office. Somehow the city and its suburbs found room for these hundreds and hundreds of officials, their families and slaves. But it is a sign of the logistical problems involved that a pair of immense stone warehouses had to be put up by Constantine on the riverside to store the town's provisions in bulk.

Constantius' reign accounted for a great deal of construction in Trèves, his son's for a great deal more. Here we touch again on the subject of the emperor's role. For, beyond the day-to-day needs of good government, the emperor was expected to travel in pomp, to surround himself with a household that proclaimed his greatness through its own swollen size, to occupy a magnificent dwelling, and to lavish his wealth on the cities where he made his home.

Trèves was laid out in a rough circle enclosing more than a hundred blocks. At its center it opened out into a

forum, on which faced the governor's mansion of the third
century and, at the opposite end, the Constantinian baths.
They were bigger than those of any other provincial
city—so large (about eight hundred feet from east to west)
that the cold-water pool alone equaled the area of the cathedral, and the exercise hall could later make a handsome
church (of SS Gervasius and Protasius). It was in one of
the steam rooms here that the empress Fausta, by her husband's orders, was later smothered. The whole gigantic
building was not the only one of its kind in Trèves. At
least one other almost as big stood near the western gates,
which Constantine renovated; but the Constantinian baths
proper were to serve the court, forming in fact a corner of
the palace complex. Three blocks to the north lay the center of this complex, marked by the still-surviving basilica
(plate VI). It dates to about 310. Originally its red brick
was hidden under plaster, painted around the windows (in
two tiers) with yellow vine tendrils and little cupids, all on
a red background. Most of the walls were pierced by pipes,
and there was a space under the floor, too, for the circulation of hot air. Forehall and nave were paved with a honey-
comb design in black and white, while geometric patterns
of many-colored marble and gilt glass covered the walls up
to the second tier of windows; above that was painted plaster, with mosaics in the vaulted space at the tops of the
windows. The apse, a throne platform in its midst, was
sheathed in gold and mosaics; over all, a gilt-coffered
ceiling. There were no columns in the 250-foot nave to de-
tract from the impression of enormous size; no interrup-
tion to the floods of light that played over the surfaces of
gold, ochre, green, red, black, and white; nothing but air,
it seemed, to support a vault a hundred feet above the floor.
One's gaze rose involuntarily into space, floated like a mote

in the stillness, rebounded from the range of colors, but came to rest inevitably at the gathering of lines in the apse. There sat or stood the emperor on ceremonial occasions for the announcement of victories, the reading of new laws, the reception of embassies. The whole building had a point. Beautiful in itself, and bringing to a focus many brilliant arts and skills, its beauty merged into the purposes of the state. It declared the power of its creator, a being who, to the awe of barbarians and peasants, could enclose so vast a space *and heat it.* Magic! such as the crusaders attributed to Byzantine emperors. And a more educated audience responded to the play of tradition and symbolism in the shape of the basilica, in its decoration, and in its use of materials.

Two blocks farther north, another section of the Constantinian palace, this the residence of the empress and the princes, was transformed into a double cathedral, in about 326. Beneath the nave of the northern half a great hall from the original structure still displays, in its coffered ceiling, frescoes of women of the royal family. They wear elaborate hairdos and jewelry. One of them is Helena (plate XA), who later sent a relic, the Cloak of the Virgin, to the bishop of Trèves to be housed in a special part of the choir. At the palace in Aquileia we have other representations of Constantine's family—his four sons as they looked in 326. Their faces were shown around the empire in gilt glass portraits, too, on glass and silver dishes, and, of course, on coins (plate XII).

From the fashions in the choice of subjects for fourth-century mosaics and paintings, we may guess that the court, like rich private citizens, spent much of its leisure in hunting. And we do not need the exquisite *diatreta* glass from Trèves—goblets of one color overlaid with a raised

lacework of glass in one or more other colors—to tell us
that there were luxurious banquets. In a twenty-thousand-
seat amphitheater one could see convicts and captives fight;
and Constantine would have been no ruler of his times if
he had not, like Diocletian in Nicomedia, Galerius in Thessalonica, and Maxentius in Rome, constructed a splendid
racetrack and stands. A panegyrist assured him it was quite
up to Maxentius'. That is what panegyrists are for. A mosaic in the palace baths shows a race in progress, and from
the same site also a glass dish painted with a similar scene
testifies to the mania for this pastime.

In summer, the whole court moved five miles out from
Trèves to a new fifty-room villa on the Moselle (plate
VIII). Here were cool or heated baths again, a spreading
residential quarter, and a most lovely view over the river;
here were the plastered exterior walls cheerfully painted
in yellows, greens, and reds; but, right in the middle the
inevitable apsidal throne hall had to be built as well. Constantine could never forget that he was emperor.

Among his drearier duties, he had to listen to reminders
of his greatness. A Gallic professor of rhetoric tells him,

How long a task it is to recount the imperial benefactions
which, returning with unmeasured abundance again and again,
replete with bounty, shine forth in such infinite number, and
so greatly favoring, that neither the multitude of them all nor
the usefulness of each could ever be forgotten through the
neglect of thanks. . . . The barbarians lie prone on the flanks
or bosom of Gaul. . . . The harvest is fruitful, provisions in
good supply. The cities are marvelously, and almost from
anew, rebuilt.

All true, no doubt; all testimony that Constantine was
accomplishing what a ruler should accomplish. Yet it is

frustrating to us not to be able to pierce through such conventional descriptions to any understanding of the emperor as a human being, in these earlier years of his reign. We must be content, instead, with the figure reflected in the mirror of panegyric or lost in the colossal dimensions of his palace. Perhaps, after all, there is a lesson here. The imperial court was what he had known from childhood, and very little else. To sit on a throne, lead armies, or offer the hem of his garment to be adored, was what he desired of all things. There may have been no rebellious individuality hidden behind all the ceremony, but rather a man happily at one with the role of colossus.

IV

THE GOD OF BATTLES

One of the few criticisms of Constantine made in the century after his death pointed at his ambition. That quality in excess is not proved by his accepting, or provoking, the army's acclamations in 306. For the eldest son of a ruler to reject his inheritance was, then as always, a step filled with danger. Once on the throne, it was only natural for him to try to build up the strength, wealth, and security of his dominions. Whatever his intentions at first, however, it became obvious within a few years that the support he enjoyed and the stability of his rule gave him the power to expand.

So much is clear. It is unfortunately much harder to determine with any concreteness just how he appealed to different interests and how those interests made their support available in a form he could use. Certainly his construction program in Trèves made him popular there, since one of his subjects emphasized it in a speech of 310. He beautified its temples and the most famous shrine of Apollo in Gaul. "According to his accustomed generosity," says a vote of thanks from Rheims, he paid for the complete renovation of that city's public baths. Independently of his aid, Arles undertook wide-scale civic improvements. The provinces subject to him present in general a picture of good health. Where local resources flagged, he investigated the cause and offered relief. At least at Autun in 311, where land had

disappeared from cultivation without disappearing from
the tax lists, and where the population as a result suffered
severely, he made a personal visit, quite disarming the magistrates. "For it is no small matter," said their spokesman,

to address the ruler of the whole world only on one's own
affairs, and in the presence of such majesty to scratch one's
head, compose one's countenance, steady one's nerves, think
up the right words, speak them confidently, leave off at the
right moment, and await an answer. In all these difficulties,
Emperor, you spared our timidity, not only in freely questioning us as to the remedies we sought but by suggesting
yourself what we did not say, while encouraging us, prone at
your feet, by your kindly words.

And by deeds: he cut away nearly a quarter of Autun's tax
obligations and remitted arrears of the previous five years.
His conduct here is reminiscent of his father; and, like him,
Constantine could surely call on his people for extraordinary contributions, in event of need, the better for having ruled them mildly in the days of their recovery.

His vigor in reconstruction extended to defense. Besides
the Cologne bridge, of great strategic importance, he
erected (in an account superlatively vague) "forts and
towers suitably placed at many points." Archeology helps
out. Constantine's hand can be detected in the military remains at Trèves, Neumagen, Gellep; Asberg on the Rhine;
Alzei, later; Yverdon, Mainz, Kreuznach, Horburg; best,
at Deutz, guarding the new bridge at Cologne. The fort
of Deutz (plate VIIA) was a square with eighteen pro-
jecting towers, including two pairs that flanked the two
gates. Its walls, twelve feet thick and sixty-five feet high,
withstood who knows what assaults in the Dark Ages,
finally to shelter a community of monks established there

in the year 1003. Testimony of the emperor's vigor in military building matches the triumphant blows he struck against the enemy beyond the Rhine in the campaigns of 306 and 310. He strengthened the fleet that patrolled the river and the Channel. All these were measures sure to arouse the loyalty and admiration of his soldiers.

While he was thus assuring to himself the sinews of war, money and men, events beyond his realm were developing chaotically. After Constantius' death Severus had been appointed by Galerius to rule in Italy and Africa, with Constantine as his subordinate. A few months later (October, 306) first Maxentius emerged in Rome as the candidate of the praetorian guard, and before the year was out, his father Maximian left the scene of his unwilling retirement in southern Italy to resume the purple at the side of his son. The capital welcomed them because of reports that it was to be subjected for the first time in history to the same taxes borne by the provinces, and because of Galerius' rumored plan to dissolve the praetorian guard. As for the army, whatever elements were present in Italy preferred Maximian to Severus. When the latter appeared on the scene, his troops began to desert, and Maximian had only to show himself in the field to secure his enemy's flight. Severus surrendered in Ravenna, and there died.

An affront to Galerius of this kind, though indirect, was certain to draw him more fully into the arena. He prepared his forces to invade Italy himself, while Maxentius and Maximian, now both claiming the title Augustus, looked around for help. Constantine was the only obvious source, and to him came Maximian, offering not only some sort of alliance, for whatever it was worth, but a stronger link to the Tetrarchy. Its prestige and popularity still stood high. Accordingly, Constantine put aside his wife Miner-

vina, recently delivered of a son Crispus, in order to marry
Maximian's daughter Fausta. She was hardly more than a
child, making the political purposes of the match quite
blatant (March, 307). In addition, he received recognition
of his title of Augustus. Secure on this flank, Maximian
went back to Italy where, in the spring (308), he and his
son for a second time triumphed, seeing Galerius' forces of
invasion melt away in desertions (April, 308), and shortly
retreat in disorder beyond the Alps.

Hardly was the danger removed than the two victors
quarreled. The older used a meeting before their army as
an occasion to snatch the purple from his son's shoulders.
Presumably a coup had been planned, but it fell through.
The soldiers shouted and raged for Maxentius, and Maximian made an ignominious exit from Rome, once more to
seek support from Constantine. There (to complete his
story) he proved no more to be trusted than a landed
shark. It is true that he met with Galerius and Diocletian
to consider a way of restoring some order to the wreckage
of the Tetrarchy, even at the price of his own second
abdication (at Carnuntum, November, 308), and that he
accepted a position as mere councillor to Constantine; but
he was not to be satisfied with the toys and trappings of
monarchy, an honor guard, free use of the state conveyances, and suchlike. When his son-in-law headed north for
campaigns beyond the Rhine, early in 310, Maximian bolted
south, seized the army treasure at Arles, and called the
garrison to his rebellion. In a flash, Constantine was on
him. It was a notable instance of the speed of movement
that a real general could exact from his troops. On their
approach, Maximian fled to Marseilles. Besieged, and offered terms, the old warrior yelled defiance and imprecations from the walls, while, unknown to him, the gates at

his back were being forced open. The city capitulated, and Maximian was disposed of—probably strangled.

Apparently in this year Constantine took over Spain. That raised him to the same eminence his father had enjoyed, as uncontested ruler of all the western provinces and legitimate Augustus. He began, too, to disentangle himself from Tetrarchic connections, now only an embarrassment. Maximian, inspired rumor said, had not been executed until discovered plotting Constantine's assassination—after which final act of treachery it was no more than proper to discard the memory of his alliance, to overthrow his statues, and to erase his name from public monuments and inscriptions. Another lineage was brought forward, tracing Constantine's descent to the emperor Claudius (268-270); another divine protector, Sol, the Sun-God, replaced Tetrarchic worships on his coins; and, traveling north to resume his campaigns on the Rhine, when he heard of the victories won there in his absence, he stopped off en route to render thanks at the chief Gallic shrine of Apollo.

What Constantine discarded, Maxentius could still use: the memory of Maximian, whose deified image received veneration on his son's coin issues. Maxentius needed all the help he could get from the living or the dead. Since stepping forward as a pretender, he had had to base his power on Rome itself, and his narrow position had begun to deteriorate. His failures and successes offer a preview of problems that Constantine was later to face. First, Maxentius' career demonstrated the degree of support that came with control of the city, mechanically, through its mint; through ranking within the Tetrarchy that the senate could influence; through a place in the heading of laws, as the first name, or the second, or any other, also influenced by the senate; and through a hold on the consulship *ordinarius* which gave a name to each year. All these were advantages of propaganda, disseminated throughout the empire, not just in Italy. The love and awe aroused by Rome reached equally widely into the corners of every province, adding extraordinary weight to pronouncements issuing from the capital. Such feelings, however, seem to have had little effect on the soldiers. It was Maximian's reputation that dissolved the armies of Severus and Galerius. With Maximian gone, Maxentius had to make do with Italian recruits, the praetorian guard, and any strength he could draw from his dominions in Africa. There a rebellion broke out (*ca.* 307), revealing the weakness of Rome. The city fed on imports. When the grain fleet from Carthage was held back and famine pinched the populace, they rioted, fought the soldiers, and opened a civilian-military split among Maxentius' subjects.

Another riot grew out of the accidental burning of the temple of Venus and Roma. This one had religious overtones. At the time, however, early in his reign, Maxentius was not unpopular with the Christian community. He suspended the decrees of persecution; he settled a disputed papacy as a police problem rather than as an excuse for hostile intervention; and when a pope was at length firmly installed, restored to him the churches and cemeteries seized by Diocletian. Yet for reasons not made clear, perhaps simply political, the Christians in Rome were glad to see the last of their ruler when his time came.

Praetorians, populace, pagans and Christians, and last in the list, great nobles, were all to be conciliated. The nobility might respond best to the rich organ tones of the Roman past, certain notes of which were sounded in the symbolism of Maxentius' coinage and acts of state. They might applaud a building program—a new temple of

Venus and Roma, a new race-course, a basilica on the
Forum Romanum, even the grand baths in the palace. But
all this cost money. Therein lies the explanation for Maxentius' harrying of the senate, whose members he killed,
whose wealth he confiscated, and whose hatred he amply
earned in his closing years, The very man who recovered
for him the African provinces (311), Rufius Volusianus,
was secretly disloyal. Many other senators stood ready to
betray him.

With the death of his little son Romulus (309), his hopes
of a future dynasty disappeared. He was thrown back on his
Tetrarchic past. That accounts for the desperation of his
recalling "The deified Maximian, my father, and the deified
Constantius, my kinsman," on the mint issues of 311. It was,
of course, the same Constantius' son that roused Maxentius'
fears and drove him to seek support in such frantic appeals
to a collapsing, or rather, already ruined, system of rule.
The clue to its collapse can be read in those same appeals,
not to any constitutional provision which might sanctify
the four-fold division of the empire, but to relationships by
blood. The distribution of power between institutions and
individuals, between the logic of the Tetrarchy and its too
human destroyers, was resuming a more traditional balance.

In Severus' place as western Augustus, Galerius had appointed Valerius Licinianus Licinius, another Illyrian soldier (plate IIB). In fact the West was quite well supplied
with rulers—the pretender in Africa, and Constantine,
Maxentius, and Maximian. Naturally, then, we do not
hear much of Licinius for some years. What does occupy
the attention of our primarily Christian sources is the tight-
ening up of the persecutions, and their dramatic remission
by the Edict of Serdica (April, 311). Nominally this latter
was Galerius' work, concurred in, or urged, or possibly

originated, by Licinius. It draws from the most fundamental wellsprings of contemporary belief (above, p. 23). The advantage and profit of the state, stressed at the outset as the reason for any kind of legislation, is traced to "the ancient laws and public order of the Romans . . . the ancestral institutions." Through religious dissension they have been neglected by both pagans and Christians. Now tolerance is granted, so that everyone "must beseech his own god on behalf of Our safety, the state's, and his own, that the state in every part may again stand secure." Prayer is patriotism, the gods directly save or destroy.

And in exultant recognition of divine destruction, Lactantius dwells on the final, horrible, lingering, maggot-infested, stinking agonies in which Galerius lay at the moment of this edict. His disease proved God's justice, driving the tyrant to acknowledge Him and to end the persecutions in remorse. The emperor died within a week (May, 311).

Shortly before, Licinius had met Constantine at Milan and had there become engaged to his half sister, Constantia. He also appointed Constantine's half brother Delmatius Master of Infantry in his westernmost provinces. The betrothal was obviously a token of political alliance, reinforcing the two parties against their respective enemies, Maxentius and Maximin Daia, who in turn responded by their own friendly negotiations. Maximin Daia's statues appeared in places of honor at Rome. Moreover, his troops and he himself at their head, on the news of Galerius' death, appeared suddenly on the Bosporus, having hurried at breakneck speed to seize Galerius' realm. Licinius gathered his own forces, and for a tense moment the two emperors confronted each other across the water. Then sanity returned. They met on a boat in midstream, and shook hands over a treaty: Maximin Daia was to rule up to the straits. He went back to Syria, there, for insurance, marrying his daughter to a surviving son of Galerius, of whom Licinius was nominal guardian. Galerius' daughter had married Maxentius many years earlier. The world's rulers were thus united in one big happy family. As Eusebius puts it,

travel by sea was impossible, nor could anyone from any port escape all kinds of torture, being racked and torn down his sides, and enduring every torment, on the chance that he was coming from the enemy of another of the opposed sections of the empire, and, being condemned, suffered crucifixion or death at the stake. Everywhere there were shields and breastplates being got ready, and provision of missiles and spears and other materiel of war, of naval ships, and the forging of weapons throughout, and not a place where people were not expecting the onset of hostilities every day.

Such was the tense and tangled situation toward the beginning of the second decade of the fourth century: Galerius recently deceased and his heritage from the Bosporus eastwards seized by Maximin Daia; Severus dead, too, and Licinius nominated to succeed him in the area from Italy as far as the Bosporus; Maximian dead, his son ruling in Italy and Africa, and Constantine supreme to the west and north. As to the lesser players, like Eutropia, Delmatius, even Helena or Fausta, virtually nothing is known of their doings or character.

But we must pick up the threads of Constantine's story, whom we left at the shrine of the Sun-God-in-Greek, so to speak, Apollo—"whom you saw, I believe, O Constantine—your Apollo accompanied by Victory holding out laureled crowns to you each of which brought presage of thirty years [of rule]. . . . And yet why do I say, 'I be-

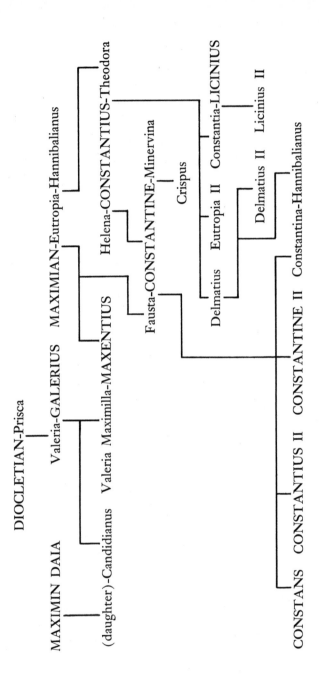

SOME TETRARCHS AND FLAVIANS

lieve'? You saw him and recognized yourself in the form
to which, as the divine verses of the seers had sung, the
reigns of all the world were destined." So declares a
rhetor in an address to the throne of mid-310. It was Constantine's first vision, described in public and to his face.

For the historian, there is nothing to be gained by dodg-
ing the account, by trying to distort it into terms he can
himself inwardly feel and understand, or by reasoning it
away. The report is a fact. In some sense also, the vision it
refers to is a fact. But it is an artistic one, the creation of a
particular culture at a particular period, as much removed
from straight sensory perception as Picasso's "Guernica"
from the news of a bombing raid in 1937. When writers of
the third or fourth century recounted the rise of men to the
throne, they naturally included, because they naturally
found in legend or written sources, or themselves thought
it only fitting to embroider, various tales of portents: to
Hadrian, auspicious predictions through the *sortes Virgili-
anae*, Sibylline verses, or the temple of Jupiter at Nice-
phorium; to Antoninus Pius, the sign of a crown
mysteriously transferred from the head of an image of the
god to his own statue; to Vespasian (in Suetonius), an apparition in a temple proffering sacred boughs and garlands.
But there is no need to multiply examples. All that must be
emphasized is the error in calling them lies (as they
would be in another culture) and the double error of looking behind them for some secular motivation. Whatever
Constantine actually saw in Apollo's shrine, it lent itself to
his role, which called for favors to be shown him by the
gods. The result, of no vast importance to him or to those
with whom he shared the account, returned to him, perhaps in heightened form, in the speech quoted above.

The deity to whom he turned, the Sun, enjoyed a greater

fame than ever before. As "The Unconquered," Sol Invictus made his presence felt on a crucial battlefield of the East, encouraging Aurelian's armies in 272. Aurelian gave thanks in his temple at Emesa and was rewarded with a direct epiphany. Soon afterwards, he erected in Rome a magnificent new home for Sol as "Lord of the Roman Empire," center of the state's chief cult, "Companion" of the throne, bestower of rule, holding out to the emperor (in a common scene of art) a globe symbolic of universal dominion. No other focus of religion could have served so well to unite under a single image all the baals of the eastern provinces—Elegabal of Emesa, Baalshamin of Palmyra, the transported Phoenician Baal Hammon of Africa, still popular around Carthage. With the most dynamic religious force in the later Empire, Mithraism, emerging on the Rhine and Danube wherever traders or soldiers traveled, Sun worship could make an easy alliance. For Mithra was the Sun, or his agent. From one of his chapels in Rome comes a characteristic inscription, embracing in one line Zeus, Helios, Sarapis, and Mithra, all honored together because all conceived of in kindred forms.

The emperor specially sought a means of attracting the loyalty of Mithra's worshippers, since they made up a large part of the army. It suited the imperial role, too, to be allied with "The Unconquered." But it would be insensitive to attribute Aurelian's religious innovations, for example, or those of his successors, solely to motives of political advantage. Certainly a private dedication to Zeus, Helios, Sarapis, and Mithra had nothing in it but genuine piety. Compare it with the similar, simultaneous honoring of "Malagbel, Bebellahamon, Benefal, and Manavat," in a Danube province—all eastern deities, all misspelled. Or take

the Rufius Volusianus who commanded on Maxentius' behalf against an African pretender. Two or three years
later he is seen in Rome holding priesthoods of Hecate, Isis,
and Sol, and described quite truly as "most pious," *religiosissimus*. He hails Constantine as Invictus. It was a common title for the emperors, a further affinity with Sol. And
finally, Cossinius Rufinus, of the same period: again, a pontifex of Sol, but also an augur, and a priest of Mars. What
moves in these men, and speaks in inscriptions from all over
the later Roman Empire, is the conviction that the heavens
have a unity. Under many names, and through many servants, a supreme being governs the whole. Chaos of Pan-
theon, impiety of myth, promiscuous confusion of a
hundred local cults—all somehow make sense, all are true,
but in a new order. Hence, no contradiction is felt in being
at one moment an official in two, three, or half-a-dozen
worships. They represent rather the different ways by
which, in an age itself *religiosissimus*, men can express the
same thoughts, as it were, in different languages.

Syncretism worked through many impulses. It broke
down divisions among various ethnic groups, it blurred the
edges of ancestral faiths. Jupiter or Jove often embodied
its compromises. It showed its force best, however, in solar
monotheism. That answered the needs not only of religion
but of philosophy. In an effort to join the two, more pro-
found thinkers of the time interpreted the Sun-God as a
being of changing manifestations. Physically, he was an
orb of light and fire in the sky, giver of life to the fields.
More abstractly, he was personified in a figure whose
acts and powers were revealed, like parables, in the details
of his life story. And by philosophers he could be grasped,
or almost grasped, as an ineffable Intelligence, infusing

light and energy into the world through his creatures, Ideas. At all levels of understanding Sol was, nevertheless, a single unifying divinity.

From him, Constantine received his throne. So said the orator. Through Sol, Constantine conquered on the Rhine in 310, and in gratitude glorified his "Companion" on his coins (plate IIIв). And when he marched toward Italy, it was, to pagans, surely that supreme being who granted a miracle.

It was on everyone's lips in Gaul that an army had been seen boasting that it was sent by divine command. . . . Your helpers suffered themselves to be seen and heard, and when they had testified to your merits, turned again from the taint of human sight. What was the beauty of their appearance, the strength of their bodies, size of their limbs, zeal of their resolution! Something terrifying flashed from their shining shields, a fearful light burnt on their heavenly arms. . . . Sent by divine command, they gloried that they fought for you.

Wonder upon wonder! lavished on their favorite by the powers above, according to the heightened expectations and fervor of his supporters.

On a more prosaic level, too, war came. Just why, seems clear from the very vagueness of our sources. Constantine wanted war, he started it, and his most ardent apologists were unable to offer any specific excuse at all for the invasion of Italy. They pleaded the sufferings of the citizens of Rome beneath a tyrant whose avarice was exceeded only by his lust. True enough, Maxentius' popularity had fallen very low, and there are hints that Constantine was invited by Romans to come to their aid. But he was not obliged to respond. Nor need he suppose that an alliance between Maxentius and Maximin Daia threatened his own dominions. Maxentius' road repairs around Trent made troop movements easier in that strategic area, but for defensive, not offensive, use. Licinius, Constantine's own ally, far from pressing him, hung back, and ended in offering no help, while Constantine's aides and generals, his very augurs, advised against a declaration of war.

In the summer of 312, however, despite all urging to the contrary, their young leader moved toward Italy. He was in his thirties, strong and confident, befriended by the gods. With him rode and marched some forty thousand. More could not be spared from Gaul without inviting barbarian invasion. The force, then, was no great armed horde, but mobile, and in large proportion drawn from the half-civilized peoples of the Rhine region. Their prowess would be needed to match the preponderance in numbers assembled under Maxentius.

He entered the peninsula by the Mont Genèvre pass, coming out near Susa. It resisted him, and he burned and burst the gates but spared the city. Next, Turin. The enemy, some in suits of mail on armored horses, the *cataphractarii*, were ranged outside the suburbs in a gigantic wedge formation. It invited encirclement, and the spectacular and impenetrable cataphracts were beaten from the saddle by maces. Milan was entered without opposition, but more enemies awaited at Brescia, fleeing after a single charge, but joining another force to make a further stand behind the walls of Verona. They were besieged, failed in a sortie, and sought reinforcements. Constantine arranged his troops in a double ring to keep the garrison in and the reinforcements out, and a desperate fight ensued, lasting into the night. With the fall of Verona, Modena, Ravenna, and Aquileia—in sum, northern Italy—came over. Constantine had not spared himself in battle, nor his troops, who stood up well to the rigors of four various encounters in a lightning campaign. At greater leisure now, deploying his fleet over the coasts farther south and around Sicily and Sardinia to cut off the African grain fleet, he advanced on Rome. It had been a hot summer.

Autumn had set in when his advance guard approached the outskirts of the capital along the Via Flaminia. They encountered contingents of the enemy and suffered losses. When the main force came up, all were regrouped; and in the pause, Constantine one night was told in a vision to paint on his soldiers' shields the sign of God, which would bring victory. It is described as the letter Chi, turned (not X but +), and the top in a loop (☥). He followed instructions, equipping a few score of his guard with the sign, we may suppose—hardly all forty thousand!

Lactantius is the source followed here. He was writing only a few years afterwards, in an eastern province but with access to court circles and to news of the West. It has indeed been argued that what we have is his manuscript somewhat brought up to date in Trèves after he had settled there. He was a devout Christian; yet he disposes of the whole miracle in thirty-one words. Pagan orators of 313 and 321, to whom we will return, speak only vaguely and briefly of divine aid to Constantine; a triumphal arch erected in 315 at the senate's orders connects the victory not with Christ but with the Sun-God. Among Christian sources, Eusebius has nothing to say about the vision in a work otherwise receptive to the miraculous (the *Ecclesiastical History* of 325), and in 336, in a long oration, he lays stress on the sign of the cross as bringer of victory, and in Constantine's presence refers to "the divine vision of the Savior which has *often* shone on you"; but he never puts

cross and visions together in any reference to the events of
312. The emperor himself ignores them in contexts where
they might naturally find a place, and an intimate of his
son's (Cyril of Jerusalem) in mid-century assures Constantius II that the sight of a cross marked in the sky by a
recent meteor is a greater grace than even the true cross
that his father found in the Holy Land. The passage, of
course, fairly cries out for mention of Constantine's vision.
Farther removed, Ambrose knew nothing of it; Rufinus
puts it in the setting of a dream. With Rufinus, we reach
the fifth century. The miracle has simply had no impact.
It has passed unnoticed among real men. But it was otherwise in the world of books, in which by this time much
fuller versions circulated.

They originated in Eusebius' effusive *Life of Constantine*, composed after the subject's death. The emperor dis-
closed "long afterwards, to the writer of this account . . .
and confirmed on oath" that, in 312, at some unspecified
spot seemingly in Gaul, and in answer to prayer, he saw the
sign of the cross blazing in the afternoon sky, and around it
the words, "In this, conquer." His entire army saw it, too.
At night, in his sleep, Christ appeared with the cross, bid-
ding him use it as a guardian. The next morning he had his
jewelers prepare a gold cross surmounted by a wreath enclosing the chrisma ☧ and supporting from the horizontal
bar an embroidered family portrait of the emperor and his
sons. This is the *labarum*.

Incontestably, the account errs in introducing the princes
into the picture; it is almost certain that the labarum as a
whole postdates 312; so also, the chrisma; and if the sky-
writing was witnessed by forty thousand men, the true
miracle lies in their unbroken silence about it. We may
compare another instance of intervention from on high. A

violent rainstorm descended once on Marcus Aurelius' enemies out of the blue and drove them off the battlefield.
This was really seen by thousands. Marcus Aurelius, on
coins and relief sculpture, advertised this proof that Jupiter
fought on his side. Why did Constantine not do likewise?
But such points of doubt did not trouble the continuators
of Eusebius' *Ecclesiastical History*. They had Constantine
discuss the portent with his retinue; they added explanation
by "some angels who were standing by," and introduced a
ring of "stars set about it in a circle like the rainbow,"
which, incidentally, removes the scene from daylight to
the night.

And ranged against the hero is the villain, Maxentius.
He, too, according to both Christian and pagan authorities,
sought divine aid through invocation of demons, consultation of the Sibylline books; through the tearing of unborn
babes from the womb for use in prognostic sacrifice; or
through the inspection of slaughtered infants' entrails.
What can be made of these stories?

In our opening chapter, the reader was warned about the
difficulties to be met with in assessing the ancient sources.
Here, by exception, a glimpse of those difficulties can be
seen arising out of the best known episode of Constantine's
career. Three elements need to be considered: what may
be called the Lactantian, the Maxentian, and the Eusebian.
The first presents us with an unembroidered psychological
event of a type perfectly familiar in scores of inscriptions
of the Roman Empire, recording some action taken *ex visu*
or *ex monitu*, according to a vision or a warning vouch-
safed to the dedicant by a god named or unnamed. Discussion of Constantine's conversion may be deferred for a
little; but there was a time before 312 when he was not, and
after when he was, a Christian. Surely it would be perverse

to deny to his dream a chief part in his change of faith. If Lactantius' account had not survived, something like it would have had to be assumed, on the model of other, epigraphic, evidence. And if there can be no certainty about the images that flashed through his sleep, we can at least believe that he recognized in them the kind of message that the divine (it was thought by Romans of the day) often communicated to men at turning points in their lives. He responded in trust. The mysterious sign which had sufficed, he knew, to vitiate the powers of Apollo's oracle and to set at naught the lore of entrail reading in Diocletian's court was borne into battle at the forefront of his army.

No test of Christianity versus paganism was involved, no crusade. Not religious systems but the strength of gods to determine victory was tested. Maxentius no doubt did make a show, as any pagan would, of conciliating the gods. What can be seen in the resulting conflict, however, is something rather submerged in the earlier Empire, and more often brought into the open in this later period, namely, the clash of magics. It is this that may be termed the Maxentian element. The essence of it, as opposed, let us say, to religious beliefs of Marcus Aurelius' time, was a sort of crudeness. People of the educated, enlightened classes in the third and fourth centuries could be detected in the conviction that they were the target of occult practices, and they responded by hiring the help of a wizard. Supernatural influences were no longer thought to exert themselves remotely, insensibly, and according only to some vague but elevated ethic. Instead, maleficence was abroad; direct physical intervention by the supernatural; apparitions and hexings, the cleansing away of howling, shrieking spirits from the possessed; apotropaic symbols laid down in the mosaic floor of a Constantinian baptistery; the prominence of the exorcist. Toward the year 312 some unknown Christian copied out on a papyrus (still in existence) the apocryphal Acts of Peter, from which can be drawn an illustration of the beliefs then circulating. It is the story of a conflict extended over several stages and in several locations, between St. Peter and Simon Magus, ending in Rome. There Christ promised St. Peter, in a nocturnal vision, "I will be present with thee when thou askest for signs and wonders." After a series of challenges and competitive displays of power, Simon announced to the multitude that he would fly.

And Peter seeing the strangeness of the sight cried unto the Lord Jesus Christ: If thou suffer this man to accomplish that which he hath set about, now will all they that have believed on thee be offended, and the signs and wonders which thou hast given them through me will not be believed: hasten thy grace, O Lord, and let him fall from the height and be disabled; and let him not die but be brought to nought, and break his leg in three places. And he fell from the height and brake his leg in three places.*

The contest between Maxentius and Constantine assumes, on a grander scale, some of the characteristics found in the triumph of St. Peter. The core of truth represented by Lactantius' brief account was dramatized by adding elements familiar to a pagan, but especially to a Christian, audience. Each party to the struggle invokes what powers he can. The outcome has the inevitability of a play. Though safety for Maxentius could have been found within the

---

*Trans. by M. R. James, *The Apocryphal New Testament* (1966), p.331f.

city, yet, in Eusebius' words, "God Himself as with chains dragged the tyrant far away from the gates."

The final elaboration appears in Eusebius' *Life of Constantine.* We may believe that much of it originated with the emperor. A sense of mission grew in him over the years. As he neared his end, that sense worked on the incidents of his life, reshaping them according to prevailing religious and literary habits of thought. He had been helped to victory by a divine visitation and a miracle in the sky. Nothing he heard in legends about other very holy men made this seem improbable. Nothing in what his contemporaries acknowledged as the facts about great events in the past or in the present, nothing in what people expected, half fearfully, from the divine, left either Constantine or Eusebius in doubt about where to look for the gift of victory over Maxentius.

On the contrary: Pagans stood ready to assure the emperor that Apollo had intended his rule, that a god— the Sun?—fought for him. Christians who knew the apocryphal Acts of Andrew had earlier read how the sign of the cross could summon to one's side God's aid in battle. Later, after 312, they might read how Constantine's son and nephew were given to see a shining cross in the heavens, visible to crowds of other witnesses as well, or might learn from the mints of a pretender how the *labarum* granted victory under the coin legend, "In this sign you will be victor." Constantine's private physician had the impudence to be converted, just like his master, through a vision of the cross to which a Voice supplied exegetical commentary, and one of Eusebius' continuators finds no cause for scepticism in the tale. Scholars who turn to the nearest department of astronomy (as some have done) for knowledge of celestial phenomena that might, in certain rare conditions, produce a cruciform light had better consult these older accounts. Constantine's miracle was a purely psychological event cast into a form dictated by the art and mythopoeia of the day.

Maxentius had enrolled deserters from Severus' and Galerius' armies, recalled regiments from Africa, and recruited in Italy. With the praetorian guard he vastly outnumbered his enemy. He considered taking his stand within the city, but instead built a bridge of boats near the stone Milvian bridge, a dozen miles up the Tiber (plate IV). He issued forth. from his gates on October 28. It was the seventh anniversary of his accession, an auspicious coincidence influencing his decision. Besides, he had more enemies in Rome than he cared to count on over a period of siege. So he marched out to clear ground, the river at his back but a double line of retreat across it ready in case of disaster.

Disaster struck promptly. It was no long affair, this historic battle. Maxentius' troops broke before the first charge, stampeded back to the river, were slaughtered in their passage, jammed the two lines of retreat, sank the bridge of boats, and died in the water. Maxentius also was brushed off the bridge and drowned. His body floated in an eddy, was noticed, and his head was cut off to decorate a pikestaff on the victor's entry into Rome. Thereafter the grisly object was sent to Africa as proof that Rome had a new master.

V

ROME, AND LICINIUS

Not for many years, perhaps never, had he seen Rome—
then as now deeply beautiful, enormous, full of meaning.
For Constantine it held not the past alone, of which events
had made him in some sense heir and master, but the present
and future as well. All time smiled on him. Without a
thought of resistance, crowds jammed the streets to catch
a glimpse of the victor, cheered themselves hoarse, and
were rewarded with scattered largesses and a good show
(plate IXA). Like our modern theater-in-the-round, a parade fairly burst with drama that all could be a part of. On
October 29, 312, the welcome of his *adventus* carried him
through the Porta Triumphalis in a coach-and-four, by a
winding progress to the start of the Via Sacra, into the
Forum Romanum, and so to his palace. The ceremony had
its rules. Thus one omission was the more striking: Constantine paid no visit to the Capitolium. But he did speak
to the people, and he met the senate. That body, with exact
enthusiasm, confirmed him in the rank of senior Augustus,
placed in his hands the nomination of consuls and other
magistrates, and protracted its thanksgivings into the next
twelvemonth by votes of a statue and an arch (plate V).
Italy voted him a golden shield and a crown for his *virtus*.
Beneath these demonstrations lay the recognition of an ir-
resistible destiny conducting him from York, only six years
earlier, to the center of the empire.

The emperor's half brothers presumably remained in their grand mansions at Toulouse, well out of sight. Nothing is known of them. In Rome, the bored and bedizened Empress Fausta received a complex of buildings on the Caelian hill, once the property of the Laterani. Here, in what never rose to the dignity of a speaking part, she dressed in jewels, had her hair curled as we see it in her portraits, and raised her children for their destiny. To the Lateran palace was added Maxentius' villa in the suburbs. To the Queen Mother Helena fell, as her quarters, a group of properties once belonging to the Sessoriani; others along the city wall; baths at the Porta Maggiore; and a villa outside on the Via Labicana. Constantine occupied the center of the center, the imperial residence sprawling across the Palatine, the "holy palace," in the language of contemporaries, or "divine house" from whose "shrine" issued "oracles" in response to "supplications."

On tiers of vaulting, which clung to the north face of the Palatine, perched palace terraces from which he could look down on the Forum. To his left, the Capitolium; to his right, dominant in the distance, the Colosseum; joining them, the Via Sacra; along it, facing him across the Forum, the temple of Maxentius' deified little Romulus, and a great new basilica, and the Temple of Venus and Roma. These structures occupied choice locations—on behalf of the enemy he had just overthrown. The senate, divining Constantine's vexation, put up his name on all three, and to the basilica, at least, he made changes sufficient to justify rededication (plates XV-XVI).

It filled a site considerably larger than a football field, reared itself 125 feet in the air, and screened its humble brickwork with a plaster exterior painted to look like the best building stone. Of its interior, little remains beyond the impression of size. A connoisseur of that quality, Napoleon, after he had restored the basilica at Trèves, turned his attention to the Maxentian-Constantinian example at Rome; but it had suffered too severely from its use as a French riding academy and drill ground. The varicolored stone floor, the geometric patterns of marble sheathing on the walls up to the second tier of windows, the painted plaster above that, the coffered ceiling, had almost all to be reconstructed in the mind's eye alone. The basilica resembled its brother at Trèves in the abundant light that poured in from the sides; it differed, however, in having two rows of eight columns running its length. At the west end, an apse. Constantine broke open the south side facing the Forum, added a porch in front with steps, and pushed out a second apse across from that new entrance, on the north side.

An apse of course brought space to a focus. Combined with ample proportions, ample light, a timber ceiling, and side columns engaged or freestanding to form side aisles, it characterized the "genus basilica" in the third and early fourth centuries. Moreover, it set off a statue of the emperor, that man himself, or his representative, some high official. Any of these figures irradiated the hall with divine majesty. In this fashion, from the confusion of uses to which a single though flexible type of building had been put, over many previous centuries, the basilica emerged as a public center for assembly and worship. Nothing could have seemed more natural, then, than to place in the west apse a seated statue of Constantine, seven times life-size, the head alone weighing eight or nine tons. It is this that now overwhelms the beholder in the Palazzo dei Conservatori (plate I).

For this statue, in the haste of the moment, pieces were

robbed from others—a hand (of Trajan?), an arm from somewhere else; not a body, which was no more than an empty shell clothed in bronze armor. Possibly the surviving head replaced, in the 320's, an earlier one recut from whatever was first available for pillage. The whole never meant to portray Constantine as he was, but rather to project the power of a god that resided in him. It held a cross in its right hand and underneath was written, "By this savior sign, the true test of bravery, I saved and freed your city from the yoke of the tyrant, and restored the senate and the Roman people, freed, to their ancient fame and splendor."

For the foot of the Via Sacra, near the Colosseum, the senate voted a triumphal arch to Constantine, completing it in 315. On it could be read the inscription, "To Imperator Caesar Flavius Constantinus Maximus Augustus, pious, fortunate, from the senate and the people of Rome, because, by a divine impulse and the greatness of his mind, with his army and his just arms, he avenged the state simultaneously on both the tyrant and all his following, this arch is dedicated, resplendent with his triumphs." And on the side panels, "To the establisher of tranquillity," "To the liberator of the city." Like his civil basilica, the arch was the last of its kind; and its decorations, like parts of the statue in the basilica, originated in other monuments frankly despoiled—of Domitian in the first century, of Trajan, Hadrian, and Marcus Aurelius in the second. Fresh sculptures were commissioned, too, notably a frieze in traditional style tracing the course of the recent war from Verona to the Milvian bridge. Two scenes, however, bear a different character. They stop the action: one, at the moment when the emperor presides over the distribution of largesses to the populace—a *liberalitas*, as coins proclaim;

the other, when he delivers a speech from the rostrum. In the *liberalitas* scene, the panel is split lengthwise in two exactly equal strips: below, tiny people turned toward the center, acclaiming him; on high, two exactly equal pairs of little galleries, each with four persons in it counting out the money; and on the platform with the emperor, five senators on the right, five senators on the left (plate IXA). In the oration scene are twenty-three figures on each side, their heads arranged neatly in two rows; behind them, an architectural backdrop of rhythmic arches and columns.

Here speak the essentials of late Roman art. As by so many more famous and more developed instances in mosaics or reliefs at Ravenna or Milan, it is the spectator who is directly addressed. Better to confront him, the chief figures are depicted full face, looking straight ahead. Crowds, retinue, arcades are laid out absolutely flat, in strings of heads all on one level and one plane, like lines of print on a page. Not the pleasure of form, but the message they convey, counts. No distraction interrupts the tableau. All within it are frozen. All of one type—whether populace, nobility, army, court, or, in Church art, saints and apostles—exactly resemble each other and are as clearly marked off from other types. Everyone has his role and uniform. But then, society too was forcibly reduced to immobility. Soldiers inherited their lot, willy-nilly; municipal senators were born to their rank and could not leave it; the peasant who fled his father's fields was brought back chained. In rhythmic prose, the laws declared what balance of the empire's strengths should be maintained, decreed their distribution in great choirs or armies or blocks of regimented resources, all to the greater glory of the emperor. He is the center; the axiality of the *liberalitas* scene repeats the axiality of his gigantic reception halls, along the length of which

march lines of columns bearing recurrent waves of vaulting, and at the end of which an apse provides the ultimate
meaning. In orchestration of art and society alike, individual differences no longer matter. They are subordinated to
function. And for that reason, a column stolen no matter
where, a carved stone medallion lifted from some predecessor's temple, any architectural element regardless of its
style or period, may be put in its appropriate place on the
Arch of Constantine.

He knew that an emperor should be a great builder, yet
he spent little time, therefore little energy, in Rome. He
left in January, 313, returned after eighteen months to
celebrate his decennalia, left again in January of 316, and
saw Rome only once more, a decade later, during a short
though important summer visit. Of his secular building we
hear very little beyond the remodeling of the Maxentian
basilica—only that he constructed public baths on the
Quirinal and beautified the portico of Maxentius' Circus
with gold leaf on the walls and columns. It was a showy
extravagance aimed at a mass audience.

Perhaps more would have been beyond the reach of his
purse. He had conducted a costly campaign without permitting his army to meet its expenses through plunder. Once
victorious, he enriched himself with no profitable pogroms
among the rich. So he found it necessary to institute a new
"lustral" tax levied in gold and silver every five years from
commerce, crafts, and professions, and a new, graduated
"glebal" tax on senatorial landholdings. The first hit the
urban poor, the second, the rural rich, roughly speaking; so
he could not be accused of playing favorites. Such henceforth regular income was supplemented in traditional ways,
including the so-called crown gold, offered to an emperor
on his accession and every five years thereafter in the shape

of a gold shield, statue, wreath, or what not. Most of this, melted down, went right to the army, but the gift from the senate in 312 seems to have been a statuette of Victory, on a globe of world rule, which was preserved in its original form on the altar of Victory in the senate chamber. It would have a rich history before it, in the coming days of Gratian and Theodosius.

A substitute for wealth was force. More and more in the later Empire the state refined a system of obligatory duties which otherwise it would have had to pay for. The principle was applied quite typically by Constantine in Rome. The city had to be fed; hungry, it was dangerous. So pork butchers who supplied city markets were dragooned into an association, a sort of guild, all of whose members passed on their occupation to their sons and to their landed property. Anyone who bought it fell subject to the duties of the guild. Similar provisions, from 314 on, constrained employees in state bakeries and grain shippers. Condemnation of criminals helped to supply the former; the ranks of the latter were filled up by drafts from the provinces. At least the shippers were rewarded with exemption from other civic obligations, and the specified quota of voyages was rotated within the guild's membership. Dedications to Constantine by suppliers of salt and by Tiberine boatmen suggest some official connection there, too, but details are lacking. All of these arrangements were called for by the free distribution of food to accredited citizens of the capital, in a tradition too ancient to revoke.

So much to please the plebs. But the emperor had another and more important constituency: the senate. It is not easy to determine its place in the empire as a whole. Certain prerogatives remained to it. They had been ignored almost with impunity by recent rulers, and, duly deferred to, bestowed no corresponding political advantage. A better approach to the question of its powers lies less in considering it as a faceless institution than as a collection of influential individuals for whom their membership provided links to a nobler age. Historically, the government of certain provinces lay with the senate—or rather, at this date, with senators, whom the emperor selected; and magistracies, from the consulship down to curators of municipal bureaus, were reserved for the same rank. So, too, the prefect of the city and "correctors" of the districts of Italy. Equestrians, that is, in rough terms, the middle class, staffed every other post. In the third century through Diocletian's reign, this had been the story, but Constantine proved a better friend.

The nearest way to the senate's heart lay through praise of the Roman past. Maxentius had named his son Romulus; Constantine, too late to match the compliment, displayed the Roman wolf on his coins (plate IIIc), emphasized his third consulship with flattering bombast and parades, and reminded the world of the capital's "ancient fame and splendor" (above, p. 84). He could fairly present himself as its liberator, in coins and inscriptions—as *Restitutor libertatis*, for example, over a picture of himself and the goddess Roma. More specifically, he liberated Maxentius' political prisoners, senators, and (the orator Nazarius is shocked to discover in jail) even persons of consular standing; he restored their property. Political accusations in the wake of the civil war, and the factious nuisance suits they bred, he tried to put an end to, with characteristically violent language. "Let the single greatest evil of human life, that detestable bane, informers, be suppressed! In their first attempts, in their very throats, let them be choked off! Let the tongue of malice be torn out by the roots! So may the judges permit neither the calumny nor the speech of the complainant, and if any informer appears, let him be subject to capital punishment."

Constantine sought the good will of the senate by opening new governmental positions to its members, even reserving certain posts to that order, and by raising senators to the rank of count. Though some of these gains were illusory, since at the same time he was drafting his equestrian supporters into the senate, he nevertheless won its friendship. He started with a popularity even predating his victory of 312, confirmed by his conduct over the next two or three years. Examples will show what his policy accomplished.

First to notice is a small group of men prominent both before and after the Milvian bridge: Aradius Rufinus, urban prefect reappointed in November, consul in 316; Rufius Volusianus, consul in 311 and again in 314, praetorian prefect in 311 and again in 321, urban prefect in 313–315; Cossinius Rufinus, proconsul of Achaea under Diocletian, holder of Roman municipal and Italian posts under Maxentius, urban prefect in 315–316, consul in 316; and Annius Anullinus, governor of Africa under Diocletian, urban prefect as nominee of Galerius, to be retained by both Maxentius and Constantine. All four were pagan, two prominently. Considering the scarcity of evidence in the first half of the fourth century, it seems fair, from this sample, to infer the presence and activity of a ponderable faction in Rome working secretly against Maxentius before his downfall and thereby earning power under his successor.

Among probable or certain family connections of these men, we know of two governors of Africa, one of whom rose to palace count, urban prefect, and (after Constan-

tine's death) consul; another, a praetorian prefect and consul of 323; an urban praetor; and a praetorian prefect of
Severus. That last surprises; yet the circle had its
appointees of Maximian as well, and at least one supporter
of Licinius. The dexterity of trimmers we may grant them,
like that of the four in the group above. We may grant that
they possessed genuine abilities. Kinship, however, is clearly
a major factor. Power reaches up the family tree of Annius
Anullinus, for example, to his grandfather holding an Ar-
val priesthood, his father a prominent senator. Aradius
Rufinus, we know, likewise could look back to notables in
two generations. And it is their habit to extend their power
to succeeding bearers of the name. Rufius Volusianus' son
was consul twice, his grandson praetorian prefect, and a
more remote descendant was St. Jerome's protegée Mel-
ania. Most famous of all are the Anicii. They begin with a
senator and proconsul of the 260's, advance to a consul and
urban prefect under Diocletian, place two brothers in the
urban prefecture late in Constantine's reign, and, like the
rest of the nobility, marry their way into still wider, more
profitable, and more brilliant alliances. They unroll their
lineage in names like Marcus Junius Caesonius Nicoma-
chus Anicius Faustus Paulinus.

Beyond kinship, wealth: Several of these families held
estates in Africa; all were large landholders in Italy. One
Anicius, urban prefect in the 320's, enjoyed fame as the
richest man of his time.

The comparative abundance of evidence concerning the
nobles of Rome makes them unique; but they especially
deserve description because they seem to be unique in no
other respect. Italy and Africa formed almost their private
domain. In Asia Minor, however, in Egypt, in Gaul, wherever we look, we find a small number of great families

similarly dominant at one time or another in the later Empire, and we may safely extend this picture to every time and province. Though the details of their relation to the emperor remain obscure, obviously politics had to take account of their friendship or hostility, had to recognize their pervasive influence in civilian administration, and had to use their talents or their protegés to fill many of the higher government offices. For Constantine, nothing could have been more essential than to win over these classes. His success may be measured in the clans that decorate Roman and Italian magistracies under his rule. Perhaps, too, there is something beyond conventional thanksgiving in the terms applied to him by Volusianus: "Our Lord, who has restored the human race, extended the Roman rule and dominance, and founded eternal security."

Security rested not only on the rule and stability of the West. In the East, the collapse of the Tetrarchy in persecutions and civil wars had yet to be completed; and from the ruins emerged a dangerous challenger.

Licinius governed from the Bosporus to the Alps, having lost Asia Minor to Maximin Daia in 311. Outwardly, all was calm. An alliance of that year continued to join Licinius and Constantine. Despite the past friendship between Maxentius and Maximin Daia, Constantine chose the latter as his fellow consul in 313. But Maximin Daia had, only a few months earlier, been at war with Armenia, a region where Christianity was especially strong. The war looked like an extension of his enmity against Christians, which he had unleashed again, in defiance of the Edict of Serdica, throughout the eastern provinces. From this period of his reign date the inspired appeals for help submitted to him by his pagan subjects. Further, a range of ingenious measures to put a better face on paganism; propaganda to vilify

Christ and Scripture; and ferocious harrying of the faithful. Those who submitted were naturally the majority,
afterwards presenting their bishops with excruciating pas-
toral problems. Who, for what degree of betrayal, and
under what penance, were to be readmitted to communion?
But there were others not in doubt, people who

have fled and been arrested, or have been betrayed by their
servants, or have otherwise lost their fortunes, or have endured torture, or have been jailed, or have shouted loudly
that they were Christians, but have been forced either by
having incense put into their hands by their persecutors, or
by having been made to swallow some food, yet constantly
protesting that they were Christians, and have always shown
their grief at what happened, in their whole bearing and
behavior and their humility of life.*

Leaving Rome in mid-January of 313 for campaigns on
the Rhine, Constantine had in his mind such reports of the
sufferings of Christians in the East. At Milan he met Licinius. What other business they had to discuss we do not
know—doubtless the terms and future implications of their
friendship, confirmed now by the marriage of Constantia
to Licinius. But chiefly they considered the plight of Christianity. Licinius, even before the Edict of Serdica, had put
about the story of his descent from the one earlier emperor
(Philip, 243–249) who could most truly be called a friend
of the Church; he had entirely ceased persecuting. Constantine, of course, was in some sense a convert. Both men
could see the political advantages to be drawn from allying
themselves with a numerous and well-organized minority
behind a potential enemy's back, though it must be empha-

---

*Trans. by A. Ehrhardt, *Framework of the New Testa-
ment Stories* (1964), 287f.

sized that there is not a single shred of direct evidence to show how this advantage really did profit them, or weaken Maximin Daia. Everything on this point must be inferred.

At any rate, what emerged in February was the "Edict" of Milan. Technically misnamed, and actually published in the East only in June, the text that Lactantius and Eusebius supply simply gives instructions to officials for the future treatment of Christians in their jurisdiction. "For long," declare the two emperors,

we have been watchful not to deny freedom of worship . . . [and] to secure reverence for the Divinity . . . so that whatever there be of the divine and celestial might be favoring and propitious to us and to all those living under our rule . . . [and] that the supreme Divinity might in all things grant us his accustomed favor and benevolence . . . [and] that the divine favor for us which we have experienced in so many matters should continue forever propitious to our success.

Let churches receive back whatever has been confiscated; let complete toleration prevail.

A curious document. The reasoning behind it fits naturally with the reasoning that induced the persecutions, namely, that the troubles of the empire arose from the anger of neglected gods. War with Armenia may have been blamed by Maximin Daia on the hostility of Christians there, in a fashion reminiscent of Diocletian's attacks against Manichaeism. A severe famine in the East in 312 certainly was laid to divine wrath by Christians, and probably pagans also, each side, as so often in earlier centuries, accusing the other of inviting disaster through omission of the due and proper cult. The Edict, then, in its peculiar emphasis on the motives for toleration, would be responding to Maximin Daia's propaganda. But still more striking is the vagueness of the Edict's theology. It tiptoes round that subject, obscuring in periphrases all differences between Christian and pagan, and, perhaps, between Constantine and Licinius. Emphasis and periphrasis together tell of conflict. It was becoming more and more a matter of general conviction that right religion controlled the public destiny, therefore more and more essential to define what that right religion might be. Trial by battle impended, and was soon to be invoked.

On first hearing of the Edict, Maximin Daia followed its injunctions grudgingly. The "worship of the gods" he valued above the "superstition" of the Christians, as he made clear in a public letter. He stressed the hallowed antiquity of the one and the narrowness of the other. At most, Christians "were to be borne with in a long-suffering and moderate spirit." Without external pressure, his involuntary change of policy could not last long, and he took prompt steps to remove that pressure. Angered at Constantine's assumption of senior rank as Maximus Augustus, alarmed by the political implications in Licinius' marriage to Constantia, and balked in his religious convictions, he took the opportunity of Licinius' involvement far away to invade his realm. The army he moved across the Bosporus was hastily collected but formidably large: Lactantius gives it as seventy thousand. For eleven days it vainly besieged Byzantium (March, 313), proceeded west at the news of Licinius' countermobilization, and encountered him in April near Hadrianople. There Licinius defeated him with a far smaller force. Maximin Daia fled, the survivors of the field deserted him. In two days he had covered the distance to Nicomedia, gathered his family, and withdrawn to the south. Vestiges of his strength blocked Licinius in the Taurus mountains. Dislodged, they opened the way to Syria. The fugitive issued a last, meaningless announcement of toleration, and shortly died. Christian accounts attribute his death to a hideous disease.

And now, with slowly gathering confidence, Christians could proclaim at last that the long night was over. They came out into the day of rejoicing, free from prison or hiding, free from fear, showing the scars of martyrdom, reassembling their lives and thoughts. An end to persecution meant much more than safety. It meant the vindication of belief. God had indeed judged their adversaries and made known His strength in their downfall. The conflict between Licinius and Maximin Daia had given proof. Looking back at the eve of Hadrianople, Lactantius could discern the tyrant vowing to Jupiter, if he won, to destroy Christianity root and branch, while Licinius, sleeping by his campfires, received a dream of an angel that dictated a prayer for victory to him. Copies were transcribed at the orders of the emperor and distributed the next morning to his troops. Before going into battle they thrice repeated, "Greatest god, we implore, holy god, we beseech thee: we commend all justice to your hands, and our safety, and our empire. Through thee we live, through thee we stand forth victorious and fortunate. Greatest, holy god, hear our prayer. We stretch our arms to thee. Hear us, holy, greatest god." It is easy to see in the words chosen the same ambiguity running through the Edict of Milan. In the ebb and flow of Christianity and paganism, this was the point of slack tide.

To Lactantius there was no ambiguity. God, invoked, had given His answer. So also to Eusebius. Speaking at the dedication of a risen church in Tyre, about a year after the battle, he pointed with passionate eloquence to "the marvelous and divine signs and acts of favor shown to men through God's wonders, made known through the reading of Holy Scripture." He quotes those passages of the Old Testament where God smites kings and chiefs; and he goes on to a description of God's opposite,

the demon who loves evil and hates good, who now, at such signs of favor and benefaction, almost burst with fury, and ranged in arms against us all his death-dealing forces, at first like a dog grinding his teeth, . . . then hissing frightfully with his serpent-sounds, now through the threats of impious despots, again through the blasphemous decrees of wicked officials; yea, more, vomiting forth his own deathliness, and with evil and soul-destroying poisons casting spells on captive souls, all but killing them.

For men of this time there was nothing remote or abstract about the contest they had witnessed. Even on the supernatural level, the antagonists were conceived of with awful vividness.

The eastern provinces were now all subject to one man. In the western, Constantine meanwhile was faced with widely scattered problems, the worst in Africa, whose story may be deferred till the next chapter, but others that called him away from Italy to put down piracy along the coast of Gaul and Spain and to drive back across the Rhine a confederacy of many tribes. Issues from the mint at his headquarters, Trèves, before the end of 313, announced victories over the Franks and Alemanni, thanks to the aid of "Sol Invictus, Our Companion" (plate IIIв).

Early in 314, Constantine, his wars over for the moment, began negotiations with Licinius to establish Bassianus as Caesar of the Italian vicariate. Bassianus was married to Constantine's half sister Anastasia. He apparently controlled certain forces already, since, when Licin-

ius tampered with his loyalty, he had the arms to turn
against his brother-in-law. Officers still loyal to Constantine, however, arrested him, and he was executed at Constantine's orders. From these events, little understood, war
broke out with Licinius. It is hard not to see Constantine,
first, as active though outmaneuvered in a trick to enrich a
puppet Caesar with some part of Licinius' realm, and second, as aggressor in actual hostilities; for, when the two
emperors fought (October, 314) it was at Cibalae, roughly
two hundred miles inside Licinius' territory. Licinius suffered defeat, withdrew pell-mell down the Save to Sirmium, evacuated that capital, and rounded upon his pursuer
in Thrace. Two brief accounts of this second confronta-
tion survive, and diverge; a hastily appointed Licinian
Caesar by the name of Valens appears on the scene, and
shortly disappears; but the upshot was a treaty, acceptable
to Licinius because of his recent defeat, and to Constantine
because of his great distance from home and reinforcements. A new demarcation gave Constantine all Europe
except the area between the lower Danube and the Aegean—
that is, Thrace. From the negotiations we have a frag-
mentary interchange between Constantine and Licinius'
emissary, at an angry moment. "Not for this," says Constantine, meaning the interposition of a Licinian Caesar,
"not for this have we come so far, not for this have we
fought from the Ocean to this point, and for this we will
not now take to alliance our brother-in-law [Licinius] for
his crimes, and repudiate our relation. We have no wish,
either, to accept a slave [Valens] into our rule." A hard man
Constantine.

VI

ROME,
AND THE CHURCH

Constantine reveals quite another character in a Church dispute developing at first beneath the surface of the persecutions, soon swelling to a confused prominence, and by 313 capable of absorbing a major part of his thoughts and energies. He might fix his eyes on the East, intently following the struggles for mastery there; he might test his strength against the winner; but during these tense times, and on into more years of distraction, he was entangled involuntarily, inextricably, and ineffectually in Donatism. There is an unusual quantity of evidence for the dispute, and an unusual value in it, for the light it sheds on the process of education by which the Roman world learned to live with a Christian ruler, and Constantine learned a little more about his fellows in the faith.

At about the time of the battle of the Milvian bridge, a council of Numidian bishops was in session, weighing the right of Caecilian to continue as bishop of Carthage, the chief city of the province of Africa (so-called *proconsularis*). Precedent in the procedure of ordination gave authority to Numidian churches over those of Africa, so that point was not the focus of dispute; rather, that Caecilian had been ordained by bishops, principally a certain Felix, who stood accused of betraying Christ in the recent persecution, and who had become *ipso facto* excommunicate. Caecilian was thus not lawfully elected; worse, though without strict legal force, he had behaved harshly toward "confessors," those who had proclaimed their faith and suffered the consequences. Immense and fervent admiration for martyrs, men and women distinct without regard to class, united the poorer folk of the metropolis with the peasants of the countryside, especially of Numidia. Caecilian's behavior cost him the support of both groups, while drawing him closer to what today might be called the Establishment— municipal senators, much of the Church directorate, the urban middle and upper classes. A split between a more forgiving and a harsher attitude toward those who betrayed Christ perplexed the Church in Asia Minor, Rome, and Egypt and called for the most delicate judgments. Here and there it produced rigorist schisms. But in Africa the same problems became entangled in wider social divisions. It was this fact which ultimately baffled reconciliation and carried the schism down into the fifth century.

It first took on institutional form with the deposition of Caecilian (which he never recognized) and the election of a successor. The latter soon died and was in turn succeeded by Donatus, from whom the schism takes its title. These steps were announced by messengers to the chief churches of the West, in Spain, in Gaul, and in Rome, where Constantine now ruled as Africa's new master.

Constantine of course set a high value on the African provinces as the source of supply for his capital. So he took precautions to win popularity by promptly proclaiming religious toleration, by rebuilding cities damaged under Maxentius, and by establishing centers for the worship of his own Flavian family and the deified Constantius. He wanted no trouble. To oversee secular administration, he dispatched the flexible Anullinus, keeping at his own side Ossius (less correctly, Hosius) of Cordova, for advice on how to handle the Church. Also present was, of course, the pope Miltiades.

Of Miltiades all that need be said is that he was no rigorist. From the part he played during and after the persecutions, one could predict an antipathy to the Donatist cause. But Ossius calls for a better introduction, since he exerted a strong influence over the emperor in ecclesiastical affairs for a space of nearly fifteen years, the most crucial in Constantine's religious development. He came from Spain, of a rich Christian family—so much we may guess from the fact that his sister also dedicated her life to the Church. Eloquent, sufficiently cultivated to receive the dedication of a work on Plato, competent in Greek, bishop of the province's largest see, and a confessor, he was marked for leadership. At the Council of Elvira (*ca.* 305?), he took a prominent hand. Sometime in 312 he joined the imperial court. He was then in his fifties, renowned for his virtue and wisdom. Doubtful sources refer to his role in confirming Constantine's conversion. It may be more useful to mention a point of view he is known to have advocated to others, therefore presumably to the emperor as well: He believed strongly in the ordered structure and protected dignity of Church government. Small wonder that Donatists came to look on him as their chief enemy.

Though these were Constantine's advisers, and though he was himself the first Christian to sit the throne, he evidently knew nothing about Donatism, neither its history nor its present state, and depended on such accounts as slowly reached him, partial in both senses of the word, to build up in his mind a picture of what had been happening in the African church. His actions in regard to his coreligionists for a brief time followed the path of Galerius and others before him, in simply reversing measures of persecution. As hostile decrees had aimed at ecclesiastical property, so now did his benevolence. The agreement with Licinius at Milan promised the return of confiscated lands and buildings; toward the same period, that is, early in 313, Constantine extended outright cash indemnities to African bishops of a list drawn up by Ossius and administered on the spot by Anullinus. A month or so later the proconsul was further authorized to exempt Caecilian's clergy from municipal obligations (*munera*).

This last favor offered really major advantages. Henceforth, those privileged could not be elected to the supervision of any of a wide range of expensive, often quite crippling, duties such as road repair, building and maintenance of public structures, oversight of town police, and, worst of all, tax collection. The collector's individual assets served as collateral or guarantee for the delivery of the sums due from the whole township. If he failed to collect them, everything he owned was sold up.

Traditional in its attention merely to the material structure of the Church, Constantine's policy also offered a traditional rationale. The views of the Edict of Milan were echoed by the letter on clerical exemption, along with a familiar ambiguity in phrasing.

Since many experiences have shown that when worship is done away with, in which is preserved the highest reverence for the celestial Divinity, great dangers afflict the state, while the same veneration, restored and secured, has afforded the greatest good fortune to Rome and a singularly happy outcome to every human undertaking, since also it is divine favors that make this true,

then let the agents of worship be privileged, etc., etc. What is new, however, and pregnant with change, is the se-

lectivity of favor. The emperor inserts himself directly
into the Christian community. In 313, for the first time in
any surviving sources, the word "catholic" is opposed to
"heretic," and by the emperor. For the first time the state
takes cognizance of an internal ecclesiastical affair. It is the
Caecilianists who receive cash grants, specifically *not* "certain persons of unsettled mind"—obviously the Donatists.
The explanation arises naturally from Constantine's quite
conservative convictions: If cult matters, then it had better
be right. As to its definition, Ossius could advise him.

The Donatists reacted instantly. It was a serious thing
for them to have their clergy discriminated against, and in
such costly ways. A crowd of them came to Anullinus on
April 15, 313, to deliver a petition. It requested Constantine to "send judges from Gaul." Another fateful step had
been taken, acknowledging, or rather for the first time
creating, the right of the state to define orthodoxy and to
punish schismatics. When Caecilian and ten of his party
joined in a deputation of their opponents for the trip to
Rome, surrender to the secular arm was ratified; and
the cooperation of Miltiades completed the process in an
unexpected way. Not only did he sit with three Gallic
bishops, as requested, but added a number of others from
Italy, transforming the tribunal into a synod and the issue
into a question of doctrine. Their orders were to inquire
into both sides and deliver judgment according to "the
most holy law." As for the source of the emperor's authority to issue such instructions, he flatly declared that any
division was intolerable "in those provinces which divine
providence has voluntarily entrusted to my devoted self."

The sessions took place in September and October, in
Fausta's Lateran palace. Judgment went against Donatus,
not only for creating division but for anabaptist views,

and he remained in Italy under some sort of house arrest. His adherents at home, nothing discouraged, continued to make trouble for the orthodox in Africa while pressing demands for a fairer hearing. They had, indeed, little substantial to offer in the way of complaint, and scandalized Constantine by their intransigent, quarrelsome language and conduct. He deplored the opportunity for ridicule that both sides afforded to a pagan audience, while continuing to hope that the issue could be resolved peacefully. Offering the services of the state transportation system, he gave orders for the holding of a grand council of western bishops at Arles in August of 314. That city's mints announced "The wisdom of our most provident emperor." In the interim, the proconsul of Africa was to try to find out more about the central point of the Donatists' accusations.

Felix, it will be remembered, could not ordain Caecilian because he himself was not in the Church, having abandoned it through surrender of copies of Scripture to the police. So said Donatists, and so they truly believed. But evidence to clinch the matter was lacking, and one of their number forged the desired documentation. This the proconsul detected, and informed Constantine. Nothing else came out of the hearings in Africa in any way damaging to Felix or Caecilian. The latter was quickly vindicated at Arles. The council, representing all of the major areas, though not all of the provinces, under Constantine, found plenty of other things to fill up its sessions, including the question of rebaptism. On this the Roman church, loser in the dispute with the African churches a half century earlier, at last triumphantly asserted its views. It was a blow to Donatus, who had consistently rebaptised both Christians who had fallen away in the persecutions (*traditores*) and

pagan converts who had been admitted to the Church by
traditores priests.

The emperor had been absent in the late summer, waging
war on Licinius. He had thus not interrogated the Donatist
forger whom he had ordered to be sent to him at Rome;
nor, of course, had he attended the council. After it ended,
however, he wrote to the bishops, commending their work
and their decision in a letter apparently drafted by some
ecclesiastic in court, Ossius or another, and declaring that
the Donatists were deserted by the Divinity, even hated of
Christ, and inspired by the Devil. Nothing else could
account for their decision to appeal from the Church to
the emperor, from a heavenly jurisdiction to a secular. On
his return to the capital in July of 315 they besieged him
with complaints and charges. They had a sort of lobbyist
or court spokesman, they had their strident selves, their
fellow schismatics at home kept writing to the capital, and
imperial officials in Africa aided their cause to the extent
at least of reporting on its wide popularity and its capacity
for disruption of the whole province. Constantine hardly
knew what to do. He thought of shipping the Donatists
back to Africa, there to appear in further hearings. A few
days later he undertook instead to conduct inquiries himself, and summoned Caecilian—who never turned up, just
why is uncertain, but perhaps because he could not reach
Rome before the impatient Constantine left for Milan (September, 315).

It is convenient to follow out the last acts of the Donatist
controversy beyond the proper bounds of this chapter. In
Milan Constantine was definitely inclining against Caecilian, until Caecilian arrived; but with attempts of the accus-
ers to slip away home, he changed his mind again. Before he

could render a decision in the presence of both parties, he was called to Trèves by news of Frankish incursions. Donatus and Caecilian evaded detention, the scene of riot and calumny shifted to Africa, and to that distracted province the emperor announced his intention of a personal visit "as the divine piety shall grant"—an idea soon abandoned, after all (early 316). In the autumn, on final investigation, he found Caecilian guiltless, and followed up his judgment within six months by confiscating Donatist churches and exiling their bishops. Carthage was wracked by violence off and on for years, until in 321 the emperor in a final *volte-face* decreed toleration, not in a spirit of forgiveness but of disgust and exhaustion.

Whoever traces the course of these events must be struck by the emperor's hesitancy in contrast with the sureness and drive he had hitherto displayed in other kinds of activity. He had traversed almost the breadth of Europe in eight years, overcoming the opposition of a barbarian king or a seasoned Tetrarch with equal confidence, and reducing every land he set foot in to his own dominion. Accommodation with Galerius, Maximian, Licinius, Maximin Daia; alliance with the image of the Tetrarchy; the aid of Hercules or Mars or Sol—all had been espoused at the right time and put aside at the right time, with the utmost political advantage. Changes of direction had been no more than tacks against the wind, still carrying him forward. In war, too, his record was unblemished. Any general may win one battle; two or three may be credited to luck and a good army; but unbroken success in a score of campaigns against enemies as different as Frankish pirates and *cataphractarii* outside Verona gave proof of real military genius. However cautious one must be in reading panegyrics, there is at least no way for them to have hidden a major defeat. Constantine suffered none. But confronted with schism, all this sureness deserts him. His board of arbiters becomes an Italian synod, and he submits; his prestige engaged in its decision, he nevertheless grants a request for a Council; the Council repudiated, he accepts an appeal to his own person; and in the next six months he inclines now to one side, now to another, now to one plan, now to another, until at last, after devoting himself to the search for a solution through every possible means, he just gives up.

These Roman years force him to step out of the role which he had chosen and played so well. An emperor he could be, in the style required by the times, triumphantly; to be a Christian was something new; and the combining of the two roles into a single whole was to occupy his formidable energy and intuition up to the day of his death. Apart from its natural difficulty, the task was complicated by the steady development of his ideas, demanding fresh answers at each stage.

At the outset of his conversion—indeed, for a long time after 312—the central question to show itself was, Conversion to what? Insistence that Constantine can never have been a real Christian because he ordered the execution of his son and wife, made war, or spoke vaingloriously, is too ridiculous, though just that insistence can be found in ancient pagan and occasionally in modern writers (the classic Burckhardt, for one). Interpretation has now long dismissed the view, also, that he invented some compromise religion, or that he feigned conversion for years before truly feeling its inner effects. These and similar distortions, however, point to something real in the history of his growth: the distance he had yet to travel, in October, 312, before attaining a conventional Christianity. Who, after all, could help him along the road? Late writers describe him, directly after his vision, rounding up a Faculty of Ethics and Exegesis, whose professors could administer a concentrated course of instruction to him. That tale need not detain us. It is more relevant to turn back to the words of a rhetor attempting to assess an emperor and being blinded by his majesty, or to various other fourth-century texts that stress the isolation of the throne, the veneration that deters criticism, the extreme delicacy called for in suggesting anything new, or detecting anything amiss, in government—"not, invincible emperor, because these matters are unfamiliar to you . . . not so much for your instruction as for your review . . . not unknown to those closest to Your Clemencies, men harassed by many cares to which I am a stranger; but preoccupied as they are, many points escape them." Such is the language of the imperial court, hardly adapted to the requirements of moral training and correction.

Clearest in Constantine's handling of Arianism over the last decade of his reign, it is nevertheless obvious, too, in the years following his vision, that he had little taste for speculation and that his religious views rested on deep but simple feelings almost independent of theology. As he could have learned from Constantius, or for that matter from Diocletian, certain of his subjects worshipped a God higher than all others, and took their name from One who taught and revealed this God; but pagans knew very little about relations between Father and Son, still less about relations between Son and man, and generally ignored the whole ethical content of Christianity; nor do these matters make any appearance in Constantine's correspondence regarding the Church. At the forefront of his mind stood only the bare conviction that the supreme power was that which Christians proclaimed, "the Supreme Divinity," "divine favor," "greatest holy God," "the divine piety," "the holiest heavenly power," "the divinity of the great God," and so on, in a dozen periphrases, all quoted at various points in the preceding pages, where we would expect the one word, "God." Writing about the Donatists in 314, Constantine mentions Christ; but several considerations, and several modern scholars, suggest that the letter was drafted or edited by churchmen in the court, not wholly by Constantine himself; otherwise he makes no reference to Christ until 321. That peculiarity deserves emphasis. It does much to explain the route that his spirit traveled in conversion, passing not instantaneously from paganism to Christianity but more subtly and insensibly from the blurred edges of one, not truly itself, to the edges of the other. Lactantius affects the same unspecific expressions, so prevalent in late antique literature. Of course, in him that shows no uncertainty; for instance, "The providence of the Supreme Divinity has borne you to the topmost heights," he assures the emperor in a dedication of about 313. But what was a trick of style for one man might control the very shape of ideas for another.

Turn next to pagans. On the arch in Rome, as we have seen, the inscription attributes victory to the impulse of the divinity (*instinctu divinitatis*); an orator of 313 demands, "What god was it, what so favoring a majesty," that inspired Constantine first to undertake a war against Maxentius? "You have for certain some secret bond with that divine mind which, delegating *our* care to the minor deities, thinks fit to show itself to you alone." As late as 321, again, Nazarius the rhetor invokes the impulse of the divinity (*divino instinctu*) to explain the marvelous deeds of the conqueror; again, he detects the operation of "heavenly favor," without source or name; and, to bring Maxentius out from the safety of the city, again Nazarius tells of the intervention of some faceless god befriending Constantine, just as Eusebius imagines how "God Himself as with chains dragged the tyrant far away from the gates" (above, p. 77).

Over the middle ground between pagan and Christian, Sol presided. It had long been common for Christian writers and artists to portray Christ as the source of light, of salvation, and of righteousness, in solar imagery (plate IIIA). To other circles, solar monotheism exerted a powerful attraction, uniting, in one whole, philosophy and a hundred scattered cults. Constantine remained loyal to Sol for more than a decade after his conversion; or at least his coins, with all the authority and perhaps the distortion of headlines in a government-controlled newspaper, continued to celebrate that god, though with diminishing honor, frequency, and emphasis, after all others had disappeared for good. As we will see in a later chapter, the emperor was slow to cut the ties with his past and with the beliefs of the majority of his subjects. The latter likewise resisted a break. Vague, evasive phrases bridging the gap between paganism and Christianity and thus facilitating spiritual movement from one to the other still served to link even such men as Anullinus to their master long after Constantine's change of faith had become perfectly clear to everybody.

Monotheism under the presidency of the Sun; a family background somewhat sympathetic to Christianity; a current religious vocabulary of circumlocutions and ambiguities; finally, the sharp impetus of his vision itself made more acute or even half-induced by the anxiety of a hazardous adventure—so many are the factors to be fitted together. If they seem complex, that is in the nature of any major psychological event, fully known; and, unsatisfactory though the sources certainly are, yet they are more complete for this than for any other conversion in antiquity before St. Augustine's. They throw light, incidentally, on quite general phenomena of the later Empire, reflected back through the language of the emperor's subjects in dissembling dedications and tactful addresses to the throne.

Behind the smoke screen is a man obliged to avoid challenge to paganism, but decidedly a Christian—on his own terms. Some compromises he will not make. He will not sacrifice at Jupiter's shrine in Rome. To do so would insult every martyr that ever died in pain. He will not admit any but the Sun-God to prominence in official art and communications. On the positive side, he will stress his ardent devotion and his deep debt to the cross. Let it be interpreted as men wished, they were at any rate to have it thrust on their consciousness that a cross had defeated Maxentius; by this sign the armies were henceforward led in battle; and with it held forward in his right hand, the emperor presented himself in the form of a gigantic statue, to the people of his new capital. Coins, too, commemorated victory with symbols obscure in their exact imagery but unmistakable in their general import: a cross surmounted by a globe on one side, balanced on the other side by his war-horse, and between, the emperor in armor, the crest of his helmet marked with Christ's monogram, the chi-rho (☧) (313? plate IIIc); in 315; again the chi-rho on his helmet, though all of these issues are rare. After 317, the chi-rho becomes more common and more fixed in shape, associated especially with the famous labarum.

What conversion meant to him, however, is better seen not in what he tried to say or show to the empire at large, but rather in the words he addressed to his coreligionists. No doubt he shocked them. If there was nothing new in the belief that an offended God might vent his wrath in punishment, Constantine seemed to carry the argument a little too far in his insistence on ending schism "lest the Highest Divinity may be aroused not only against the human race, but even against me, myself, to whose care, by His decree, He entrusted the governance of all things here below." Schism was detestable, all would agree, but, to Constantine, "unbefitting to the Divinity and to my good repute." To bishops, he alternates the most flattering salutations—"most honored," "dearest brethren"—with a tone of imperious impatience more suited to an audience of minor bureaucrats; and whatever hand he had in the phrasing of a letter already referred to, it is quite untypical. There he confesses his own previous state of sin and the divine mercy that enlightened and forgave him. He humbly awaits judgment himself, who is appealed to as judge. An unexceptionable way of looking at things. But after that admission or disclaimer he goes right ahead with his judging—even grows in the role as he begins to feel better informed about the meaning of the faith, and by 315, in the midst of threats to visit Africa personally, promises to "make perfectly clear to everybody what, and what sort of, cult must be offered to the supreme Divinity and in what kind of worship He seems to take delight." The spirit of violent didacticism of course contradicts the emperor's position—one may say, his entire lack of position—within the Church. Moreover, it contradicts his chief intent, harmony; hence, more than from any real or pretended humility, he seems to shift indecisively from one stance to another. As early as 313 the key word "concord" (in Greek, *homonoia*) has entered his correspondence; as late as 321, when he washes his hands of the dispute, *homonoia* has yet to be achieved. No amount of force could make men feel like brothers.

For his part, Constantine could not lower himself to a genuinely fraternal level with mere common citizens, hardly, indeed, with bishops. Some position far higher than that of other members of the Church had to be found for him. Was he to be truly inside, and therefore subordinate to episcopal authority? That would not do, surely. Yet he could not be left outside, either. While answers were being sought to puzzling questions of his status, slowly to evolve through accident and precedent, he could at least express his benevolence in that most traditional of roles, as a builder. Every other great emperor, every great king, had left a mark of stone on history.

Except for a parish church or two, late in his reign, he built nothing for Roman Christians within the city. It would have cost him too dearly in loyalty among his pagan subjects, for whom—and especially for the great nobles— the capital's religious heritage meant everything that was dearest, most holy, and sacrosanct. Beyond the walls, however, these associations faded away; others of a different nature enshrined places of martyrdom; and, if only as a minor consideration, land was more available. Here rose San Giovanni in Laterano and a half-dozen other magnificent structures.

Once more, though quite irrelevantly, we encounter the equestrian statue of Marcus Aurelius. Before being moved to its present location (above, p. 1), it stood, under the strange medieval name of "Constantine's Horse," near the house of Marcus Aurelius' grandfather, where the boy grew up; there it still stood when the property passed into the hands of the Laterani, and afterwards became Fausta's.

By late 312 or 313 she had offered the house as permanent papal residence, and in one of its halls Miltiades and his fellow bishops listened to the charges and countercharges of Donatus and Caecilian. Close by, on the site of the barracks of the horse guards (*equites singulares*) who had resisted Constantine and were dissolved in punishment, a great church was built. Construction began in 312 or 313 and ended in 320. When complete, it measured 250 by 180 feet, with a height of 100 feet. Down its length ran two pairs of aisles split by rows of twenty-two columns (plate XIII). The nave was flanked by two lines of fifteen columns and ended in an apse holding an enthroned statue of Christ and four angels, of purest silver, with jewels for eyes. Big enough to contain several thousand people, the cathedral was grand enough to overwhelm them, too. Gold sheathed the apse; columns were of rare green, red, and yellow marbles; gold glittered again high above on the beams, and from no less than seven solid altars; mosaics lined the underside of the intercolumnar arches. Across the sanctuary stretched a silver screen. When light failed from the windows, six gold and silver candlesticks and one hundred and fifteen candelabras could be lit.

In the same papal complex stood a baptistery of incredible luxury, lined throughout with porphyry and containing, among other costly objects, a solid silver font, a solid gold candelabra of 52 pounds on a gold platter, itself on a porphyry column; and sculptured silver statues of such figures as Christ and St. John, with weights specified: 170 pounds, 80, 125. Baptistery, palace, and cathedral set off the pope with a unique and enumerated splendor suitable to his eminence in the western empire and expressed in a language of universal meaning. Herodotus would have understood, or Croesus of Lydia, or the priests of Apollo to whose shrine the king gave "two big, big mixing bowls, a gold and a silver . . . of which the gold now lies in the Clazomenian vault weighing 8½ talents 12 mnai, the silver at the corner of the forecourt, having a 5400-gallon capacity." Priests in the Lateran kept just the same kind of minutely particular accounts, testifying, all but a very few items, to the emperor's estimation of the papal dignity. It was weighed and not found wanting.

Over St. Peter's tomb Constantine erected another basilica, later in his reign (beginning 324–330). Because of the importance of the site, provisions had to be made for extraordinary crowds. A part of the Vatican hill was carved away and transported as fill to a lower part to form a terrace. Elsewhere, on the Via Nomentana, rose Sant'Agnese. Constantine's daughter Constantina owned and donated the site. On the road to Ostia, the emperor built San Paolo; on the imperial estates called Sessorian he built Santa Croce in Gerusalemme, where once sprawled an imperial villa of a century earlier, and to which Helena gave both the land and a relic of the True Cross. Her son honored martyrs of the Great Persecution with the church of SS. Marcellino e Pietro, of about 314, and a martyr of the 260's, with San Lorenzo. But the list grows tedious. Such a campaign of construction, surrounding the city with a circle of jewels like a tiara, had not been seen within men's memories.

Something should be said of the wealth lavished on these structures beyond their initial cost. What must have constituted a large portion of the imperial landholdings around Rome and elsewhere in Italy, accumulated over centuries of inheritance and confiscation, passed into the hands of the pope as endowments: not less than a hundred *fundi*, as they were called—estates—of which some amounted to whole townships, and from which an income of some thirty-five

thousand *solidi*, perhaps two and a half million dollars, resulted annually.* In a long catalogue of articles for decoration and divine service, of staggering generosity, the emperor presented these Roman churches with well over a
ton of gold, to say nothing of nearly ten tons of silver in
the same various forms, as cups, statuettes, candlesticks,
etc., plus scented oils, perfumes, incense, spice, papyrus,
and balsam.

With only slightly less magnificence the imperial treasury bore the expense of the construction and endowment
of basilicas in the Alban hills, not far from Rome; at
Capua, Naples, Milan, and Aquileia, in Italy; at Trèves; and
at Cirta, in Africa. The dates of these gifts (at Cirta, as
late as 330) often carry us beyond the Roman years, or
stretch out from their origins into a decade or more of
labor and decoration. For all that, they may betray signs
of haste. San Pietro simply incorporated parts of the ad-
joining circus of Caligula and Nero. Its 136 columns, no
two alike, were torn from buildings put up by half-a-dozen
previous rulers, while other basilicas of Italy made partial
use of the foundations of imperial villas, or barracks, or
palaces. The process recalls the extensive pillage that supplied sculptures to the Arch of Constantine. In so different
an undertaking as his fortress at Alzei on the Rhine, pillage
meets us once more. Buildings half finished are rededicated
or put to a different use. A pattern emerges. It expresses a
vaunting, strident, overambitious stretching of resources,

---

* In Constantine's time, 72 gold *solidi* weighed one pound.
A heavy cloak might cost 2/3 *sol.* or less; a man's food for a
year, 3 *sol.*; a horse, 1 *sol.* or less. Equivalences are virtually
impossible to draw, but if one must be offered, it might be
1 sol. = $75.

a determination to recover, in the name of the builder, all the grandeur that once arose so effortlessly throughout the empire from sheer plenitude. The same straining for effect marks the literary style of the epoch—but words come cheap.

If Constantine seemed to be using up too much of the empire's strength too fast, in the remarkable patronage that he extended to the Church in Rome and to many farther areas of the West as well, yet in the process he laid the foundations for something of the first importance. The basilical church came into being in his reign. It was he that multiplied examples of it, to make it, where otherwise local styles would have developed, a predominant type destined for long, long life, even to the present day. Less vigor, or a later Christian emperor, might have produced a different structure for religious services—let us say, for example, a brick-vaulted polygon opening off the center of a lengthy stoa. But perhaps hypothetical history is not worth writing.

The basilica was chosen not by any one architect, not by the emperor, not by the pope, but by the very times. In 200, an odeon, in 400, an octagon, might have suggested a shape to accommodate the community's needs for religious assembly. Temples, of course, could supply no model. Quite apart from their hateful associations, they were houses for gods, not for men. Particular developments, however, pointed to the actual answer. The monarchical bishop, and the formality of the later third and fourth century that characterized what he did and wore and said, required some axial arrangement to focus attention on him. Enthroned in the apse, he resembled the magistrates who had for centuries presided in secular basilicas; and as God's throne room, the basilical church could be called, in literature or dedicatory inscription, an *aula,* just like the imperial audience hall. Hence the parallels between, for example, the secular Constantinian basilicas in Trèves and Rome and San Giovanni. The resemblances are close, but not exact: not in the development of the transept, not in the aisles (lacking at Trèves), not, alas for the modern tourist, in the heating arrangements; but identical in other broad aspects of plan and construction, especially in unsparing resplendence and varicolored, light-flooded glitter.

Inevitably the officers of the Church adopted certain distinctive features of secular officialdom for their costumes, for processions, and for address. Inevitably they presided over worship in surroundings reminiscent of a palace; increasingly in Christian art Christ borrows the ceremonial of imperial reception, oration, and *adventus* scenes. The Church, thanks to Constantine, had attained a new wealth and public prominence. To express it, there was only one obvious language of magnificence, the language of the imperial cult and court. But in that fact was implicit the danger of a friend becoming a master.

VII

EASTWARD

The decade between Constantine's first peaceful settlement and final military conclusion with Licinius (324) carried him on wide travels. At the end of a six-month stay (July, 315–January, 316) in Rome, he abandoned that city as his chief place of resort. Aquileia, at the head of the Adriatic, replaced it during most of 318, but thereafter saw him no more, and the palace built there by Maximian was given for a church. Milan he visited in 316, and, in the same period, certain Gallic cities, and Trèves; but never again. Except for the return to Aquileia, he had turned his back on the West as early as 317. The centers where he wintered, or between which his constant journeying lay, were, in order of their importance to him, Sirmium (Mitrovica on the Save), Serdica (Sofia), and Thessalonica (Salonika). Siscia he visited also, and his birthplace, Naissus, which he beautified and renovated. At Naissus the main route from Aquileia and Sirmium divided, one fork going down to Thessalonica, the other to Serdica and thence to the Bosporus. Geography pointed to politics. Though not in itself warlike or a breach of agreement, Constantine's hovering on his flanks must have made Licinius nervous. Its ultimate tendency was all too plain.

Licinius had tidied up his realm by a half-dozen murders in 313 and 314: Valeria, Galerius' wife and Diocletian's daughter, was killed; Prisca, Diocletian's wife; Candidianus,

Galerius' son; and Severus' son and Maximin Daia's son and daughter. No figure or figurehead remained in which dissatisfaction could find a focus, and a policy of religious toleration simultaneously acted as a sedative. All was quiet as sleep or death in the eastern provinces. In consequence, our sources have very little to say about them, except in so far as their ruler took a part, and a pacific one, in Constantine's doings. The two rivals were joint consuls for 315, and three of their children by agreement were promoted and mutually recognized as Caesars in 317: Licinius II and Constantine's eldest son, Crispus (both young men, the latter born in 303), and the tiny Constantine II (born 316?). Fausta produced a second son in the same year, Constantius II. In the next, Licinius and Crispus were consuls; in 319, tit for tat, Constantine and Licinius II; but in 320, two members of the same family, Constantine I and II; again, in 321, Crispus and his half brother Constantine II. The next year, Licinius balked. He could not prevent two nobles being nominated to the office in Rome, but in his own part of the world he and his son proclaimed themselves consuls. The decision had an obvious significance. It was a declaration of estrangement. A little more was at stake, too. The position of Caesar and subsequently of consul brought to public attention a second generation in each ruling house, whose prominence served to buttress the larger structure of their fathers' fame. For the Augustuses it was desirable to advertise their sons and train them to high office and public appearances. Hence the importance of the magistracy that gave a name to each Roman year.

Crispus was present when Constantine celebrated the beginning of his tenth year of rule in July, 315, at Trèves. After a second sojourn in the West, his father left him on his own in 318—or rather, not quite on his own, since he was only fourteen, but with the staunch Vettius Rufinus as praetorian prefect to guide and advise him. A certain Acilius Severus succeeded Rufinus (322–324). The arrangement anticipated the so-called regional prefectures to develop later (above, p. 47). In the winter of 320, with the incredible rapidity of movement even through snow and ice, the heroic prowess, and the personal bravery in battle that panegyrists can always discover, Crispus defeated the Alemanni and Franks, and centers for the emission of money in Sirmium and elsewhere repeated to the Balkan regions the news joyfully brought from the West (plate XIIc). For the entrance of his father on his fifteenth, and himself on his fifth, year of rule, Crispus came to Sirmium, there to be shown off to the *comitatenses* and there to take a wife; and after his return to Trèves, in 322, a child was born to him. Constantine expressed his pride and happiness through a general amnesty to all criminals "except enchanters, murderers, and adulterers," those being beyond the pale. The list throws an interesting light on morals and mores of the time.

During this period of his life, Crispus' own young morals were in charge of the septuagenarian but still vigorous Lactantius, whose name, as the historian of the persecutions, has often appeared in earlier pages. Much by Lactantius, but little about him, survives. He began as a student of Latin rhetoric in Africa, emigrated to Bithynia, set up as a teacher, and, not attracting enough pupils to occupy his time, turned to the composition of a great work in defense of Christianity, the *Divine Institutes*. Books I and VII brought him to the attention of Constantine through rather lengthy, heartfelt passages of dedication and praise, proclaiming that "God the Highest raised you to the blessed heights of rule; you then made your resplendent beginning

as savior to all and ruler most desired, restoring an overthrown and subverted justice and cleansing away the dark-
est crimes of others, in reward for which God will grant
you happiness, virtue, and long life."

These were views with which Constantine could not
fail to agree; but he must have found other qualities in the
book sympathetic also. Its author indeed knew Plato, Aris-
totle, and Pythagoras, but not at all deeply. His was not a
subtle, teasing ingenuity. He wanted to be clear and to
persuade—exactly the aims to which the emperor would
quite naturally respond. The mysteries of the triune God,
for example, Lactantius simplified, first by ignoring the
Holy Ghost, and then by an analogy with a most ancient
point of Roman law, *patria potestas:* "When someone," he
says, "has a specially beloved son, who, however, is still at
home under paternal authority, the son may grant to his
father the name and power of 'Master,' but in civil law it
is one household and has one master. In the same way, the
world is one house of God; and Father and Son who dwell
in concord in the world are one God; for the one is as two,
and the two are as one." It was, in theological terms, an old-
fashioned, Latin-Western binitarianism, made plain by an
illustration from family life. Though Greeks might scorn
its superficiality, every Roman would find the style of
thought attractive. So also Lactantius' moral views. When
he thinks of villains, he thinks of "a brigand, an adulterer,
an enchanter, a murderer," more than once held up to
execration in the same list as Constantine's. And, in a chapter characteristically quoting Vergil, Lactantius' favorite
poet, every Roman could grasp another metaphor that the
Latin Fathers, not the Greek, enjoyed using as explanation
of a Christian's role.

For he who keeps faith with his king in military service on this earth and with some outstanding deed, if he survives, is the more acceptable and dearer, and if he dies, attains the highest glory because he met death for his leader. How much more, then, should we keep faith with God the commander of all.

Thus throughout this life, since God has provided an adversary [the Devil] for us that we might gain moral strength, we should abandon present pleasure lest the enemy subdue us. We should watch and stand guard, submit to military campaigns, shed the last drop of blood, and in short bear patiently every bitter ill, the more readily because our commander-God has established eternal rewards for our labors.

Against man is ranged another army, under another commander, a "demonic" one that seeks to destroy the faithful through divisive and misguided heresies. Search for salvation must struggle forward in arms, just as Constantine had advanced from York to Sirmium.

Perhaps we may detect Lactantius' influence in the promotion of his friend Severus to praetorian prefect in 322, consul in 323, and prefect of Rome in 325. The man was a mere equestrian by origin, and a Spaniard, which would not help him. Certainly it gave signal proof of the trust placed in Lactantius that he became adviser and teacher of Crispus. But there are echoes of his thought in Constantine, making it useful to mention a few of his views as windows on the emperor's mind. It may have been from Lactantius that he picked up a fondness for thinking of God as an impersonal diety, a *numen,* to which fitted the monotheism of the solar cult and some of the symbolism on the arch in Rome; compare, too, Lactantius' description of God as

Sun, heavenly light, and so on. Like Lactantius, Constantine quotes the Sibyllines, and sketches the logical necessity for monotheism and the origin of the human race in clearly Lactantian terms. When Eusebius speaks of the emperor "passing sleepless nights in equipping his mind with divine knowledge," we may imagine him reading the *Divine Institutes*.

Vettius Rufinus and Severus in Gaul, other carefully chosen men in Africa and Italy, and Constantine over all, fostered the prosperity of the West in every way they could, by keeping out invaders, dispensing evenhanded justice, and promoting the physical well-being especially of the cities. The orator Nazarius, speaking in Rome in 321 and mentioning plaintively how long the ancient capital has been deserted by the court, cheers up at the thought of "barbarians lying supine around the flanks or in the very heart of the Gallic provinces . . . ; [there are] abundant provisions and ample harvests. The cities are marvelously embellished, almost refounded entirely." The same year gave the explanation: tireless supervision. A law forbade anyone to despoil public buildings of ornaments, marble, or columns; and a directive to the praetorian prefect, evidently following similar orders in previous years, vigorously rebukes "the negligence of provincial governors, who have put off imperial commands," sometimes beginning public works without completing them, and who are to report immediately to special building inspectors sent out from headquarters.

In the ranks of the civil service would now be found Christians, in far greater numbers than before the Great Persecutions. As a gesture of confidence in the new regime, the Council of Arles had laid down guidelines according to which state officials could remain fully within the body of the Church. Such a one was Acilius Severus. His many letters to and from Lactantius make clear his Christianity— but therewith, a difficulty that the emperor must face. When Severus was serving as vicar of the praetorian prefect of Italy in 318, many leaders of paganism must have felt a sense of shock. True, the Diocese of Italy had been, since Diocletian's reforms, actually divided into two regions, a northern or "annonarian" administered from Milan, and a "suburbicarian" south of the Rubicon, administered from Rome. Paganism at its heart remained in some degree independent and protected from the central authorities, until 321. It was then that Constantine cut back the Rome-centered administration to a hundred-mile circle around the city. The authority of its magistrates over the rich lands of Campania or Etruria or Sicily, where many of them owned farms and handsome villas, thus vanished. And worse was still to come. In 323 Severus became the first Christian consul; in 325, as the final outrage, he was appointed urban prefect. By successive and unmistakable encroachments on the religion and political independence of the Roman nobility, the emperor had indicated his growing indifference to all that the ancient capital stood for. An alliance cemented in 312 between the throne and the aristocracy broke apart.

Another set of facts illustrates the estrangement. It concerns the procedures, private and public, for making contact with supernatural forces. Pagans of course believed in magic; so did Christians as well, solemnly forbidding homicide by hexing, at the Council of Elvira where Ossius took so prominent a part; forbidding divination, "cleansing," or cures by magic, at the Council of Ancyra some years later (*ca.* 314). The reasons were plain. As Lactantius said in the *Divine Institutes,* "astrology and the consultation of

haruspices and augurs are inventions of demons." Constantine, however, assumed a more ambiguous position. He
legislated against black magic while continuing to tolerate,
even to authorize, invocations of benevolent forces. His
stance caused confusion and resentment. In 318 he threatened to burn alive "any *haruspex* or priest or servant of
these rites" who entered a private house. Perhaps the wording seemed to challenge all cults whatsoever. In an extraordinary appeal against this decree, the urban prefect,
Septimius Bassus, hurried north to the court at Aquileia.
The emperor yielded, to the extent of defining his will
through a series of further laws. One, addressed to Bassus,
distinguished, on the one hand, between incantations aimed
at injuring another person's life or virtue, and, on the other
hand, good spells for medicinal purposes or "those aids in-
nocently resorted to in country districts to avert storms
from the ripe vintage or stones of downrushing hail—
spells harming no one's health or repute but salutary in their
action and preserving the divine gifts and men's labor from
destruction." A second law of 319 dealt with divination,
terming it "a wrongful usage of the past"; a third, of 320,
contemptuously calls it "superstition." Yet in that same
year lightning struck the Colosseum; officials reported the
fact and the diviners' interpretation to the court at Serdica,
and Constantine answered the urban prefect, Maximus,
with a law ordering that the same steps should be taken in
the future whenever the palace or a public building was
struck. "Written records thereof shall be very carefully
collected and referred to Our Wisdom."

Without raising Constantine from the grave to face our
questioning, we cannot disentangle the details of his reasoning in these various decisions. They illustrate, however, the
operation of two factors already familiar in the context of

his conversion: politics and personal faith, often at variance
with each other. He must not alienate the pagan masses,
much less the great pagan families of Rome, whose wealth
was scattered through so many lands and ventures and
whose influence spread so deeply into government. The
successor of Bassus in the urban prefecture, Maximus, was
a relation by marriage of Constantine's brother; we may
count on such a person to have weight at court. Yet at the
same time, Ossius, and Lactantius through his writings, and
men and books unknown to us, were doubtless seeking to
clarify and strengthen the emperor's Christianity. No effort could dislodge his belief, shared ubiquitously by people of every faith, that the Supreme Divinity did not rule
alone or unchallenged in the heavens. "Lesser gods" and
"demons" made their presence felt. Concession might be
made to their misguided worshippers. For peace and security, the state might even officially recognize them, and permit the conciliation of forces manifest in hailstorms and
thunderbolts. Constantine granted these their power. But
it was not the *Supreme* Power, that much he knew for
certain. He could not hide his scorn of paganism for error
on this, the essential point. And this is what divided him
increasingly from the Maximi, the Septimii Bassi, and their
like.

How it must have hurt them to see their place in leadership usurped by clergy! For in this period of the reign,
money poured into church building, attention was distracted from the ancient concerns of the throne to obscure,
if nevertheless dangerous, disputes in Africa, and legislation
settled on the upstart aristocracy of the new faith a range
of valuable privileges and powers. We will return to these
later. They indicated how closely Constantine had come to
identify his interests with Christianity, even with God's

will. God, he believed, meant him to rule, meant him to
conquer at the Milvian bridge, gave him victory in all his
undertakings, and looked with favor on his efforts to secure
the unity and peace of His Church. In exchange, if indeed
he saw it as a bargain, he was to stand behind the true
doctrine and the fullest possible authority of bishops, insur-
ing to God acceptable worship.

His rival to the east, Licinius, in contrast, had never
been a Christian, but he seems to have been no fanatic pagan, either. At least he had joined in the Edict of Milan
without demur, and practised toleration thereafter. It is
surprising to find him in 320, as Eusebius puts it, abruptly
revealing the character of "some terrible wild beast or
winding snake that coils about itself." First he dismissed
from his household staff all who would not sacrifice to the
gods; next, soldiers— including (in an account that happens
to survive) a man whose father had died a martyr under
Maximian. History repeats itself. The familiar edicts were
posted in public places, the familiar laws forbade divine
services and instruction. Churches were locked up or razed,
episcopal synods banned, and, after a while, bishops im-
prisoned. Here and there, more on local initiative than re-
flecting any general order, a few martyrs died. But the
assault on the faithful never bore the all-out character of
earlier persecutions. Probably it struck only where Licinius himself appeared or where some overzealous governor
exceeded orders. And there were puzzling inconsistencies.
Licinius' Christian wife retained influence sufficient to protect her friends among the clergy, notably the bishop of
Nicomedia, Eusebius (not the historian), who not only
continued to move about freely but even to act as Licinius'
secret agent on an embassy to Constantine.

Contemporaries offered no real explanation for the suddenly ardent piety of Licinius, and modern conjecture must supply the deficiency by attributing the change of policy in the East to opposite changes in the West. The further Constantine's sympathies moved in one direction, the further his adversary's had to move in the other. It is a fairly satisfactory line of reasoning. No doubt rightly, it leaves to Constantine the initiative in a developing tension, on the model of events of 314. He had, moreover, taken to using Serdica as his chief base, closer to his enemy's borders than Sirmium; and it was his troops that made the first move. Perhaps the troops hold the answer. Constantine's were very predominantly pagan. They shouted to him, "The gods preserve you!" (note the plural), and coin issues bore the more obviously pagan legends, the more certainly they were intended for army pay or donatives— at least up to the very brink of conflict. Then concession ended. Sol, declining from 320, finally sank in 322, whereas Licinius at about the same time was establishing November 18 as a day on which the armies of his western flank were to celebrate the rites of the Sun en masse, and on his coinage offered for veneration Jupiter the Savior. If his rival's religious preference spoke to Christians—that is, mostly civilians, and Romanized or Hellenized—in Licinius' own realm, then Licinius must obviously appeal to pagans—mostly soldiers and barbarians—in Constantine's army. Such, at any rate, was the logic of the situation.

Contact between the two halves of the empire fizzled out in reproaches, distrust, and charges of plots and bad faith. These overlapped with the period of mobilization, for war was long in preparation. Licinius tightened the screws of taxation to fill his treasury, thereby causing much complaint and diminishing his popularity among his people; Constantine, to assemble an army, drew detachments from areas near the front, affording a weakened flank to barbarian invasion. King Rausimodus, in consequence, led his Sarmatians across the Danube into Pannonia in the spring of 322. He had not penetrated far into the province, however, and was held up by the siege of some city, when the Romans surprised him, drove him back to his kingdom, pursued him even there, north of the Danube, and brought him to bay. He died in defeat and Constantine returned home victorious. A venturesome young poet, Optatianus Porphyrius, who had been on the campaign, celebrated it in verse, and the mints worked overtime: "Sarmatia Conquered," "Sarmatian Triumphal Games." Booty was distributed in June, the hordes of captives scattered as slaves and tenants in the lower Danube lands.

But still the region knew no peace. When the river froze in January, 323, the Goths poured over it into Moesia and Thrace. Once again Constantine took the field to clear the empire of its enemies, and subsequently laid down regulations for a better defense, punishing civilian collaborators who aided barbarian raids and garrison officers who granted too generous furloughs when such raids impended.

A different reaction to the crisis came from Licinius. He complained that Constantine's rescue operations had violated his territory; and this was the ultimate, formal excuse for the declaration of war.

For a really complete, consuming, unreserved effort at slaughter and destruction, there is nothing to match a civil war. This one engaged armies bigger than any seen since the second century, and not to be seen again for a thousand years. It not only drew methodically on the resources of both East and West but, from the outset, promised activity on the sea as well as on land. That was implicit in the Bosporus; and that was why a harbor was made ready at

Thessalonica, using the labor of Gothic prisoners of war, to fit out and accommodate 200 naval vessels, 2000 transports, and thousands upon thousands of rowers and sailors. The army of Constantine grew to 130,000, while Licinius, for his part, scoured his dominions with equal thoroughness to gather 165,000 and a navy of 350 ships.

By 324, when fighting began, the conflict had taken on the character of a crusade. For Constantine, the battle cry was not legitimacy, though indeed he was the senior Augustus and though he now dusted off the memories of his ties with Maximian; it was not his just claim to have defended the realm where his rival proved incapable; rather he emphasized the need to rescue his coreligionists from the oppression of a tyrant. His determination was insolently implied in a recent piece of legislation directed against anyone who forced Christians to perform pagan sacrifices. Such a person was to be beaten in public; if of a high rank, to be fined; if a fellow emperor (we may add), to be made war on. God would aid the cause. For some time, now, Constantine before every battle had retired into a portable chapel a distance from camp, where he would pray for victory; and, Eusebius tells us, he never had to wait long to be honored with the Divine presence. Inspired, he would rush from the tent to lead his soldiers. They would be drawn up awaiting him, at their head a picked squad of fifty around the *labarum*. Constantine found the holy standard so effective in the war against Licinius that he directed its powers, "like some triumphant amulet against mischance," wherever the enemy seemed near to winning. He related to Eusebius how, in particular, a sudden panic induced one bearer to throw it down, only himself to receive a prompt and mortal wound in the belly. The man who took his place saw to his astonishment that every

arrow aimed at him stuck instead into the slender shaft of
the *labarum*. In fact, no one who bore it was ever hit.
Later, the emperor commissioned a painting that hung
over the palace entrance, showing himself and his children,
and beneath them, pierced by a spear, the Devil in the form
of "a dragon and a twisting serpent." The picture is explained by contemporary coins (*ca.* 326) on which the
labarum, with portraits of the three Caesars, skewers a
snake on the ground; and in turn the coins are explained by
the likening of Licinius to a serpent. The ancient imagery
of evil was here newly applied to depict Licinius as the
Devil incarnate, while Constantine, of course, fought for
God, and God for him.

One final miracle: During mobilization of the eastern
provinces, units of Constantine's army were reported
marching, as in triumph, through the cities—an apparition
sent by some power from above. Readers will recall those
supernatural soldiers that joined Constantine, according to
a pagan source, on his way south against Maxentius. It was
characteristic of this age far more than of any other within
memory, that the gods should manifest themselves directly.
Thus in a battle fought out on a higher plane simultaneously
with the earthly, transforming the whole into a cosmic
struggle between good and evil, opinion inevitably opposed
to Constantine and his God not merely a human adversary,
but a divine as well. Licinius, like Maxentius in Rome, was
portrayed at the center of a group of diviners, wizards,
seers, priests, and prophets. Sacrifices returned a promise
of victory, oracles blessed his enterprise. On the point of
engaging with his enemy, he called aside his nearest supporters to a shrine. There he delivered a speech repeated to
Eusebius by an eyewitness, in which Licinius contrasted
the new and old, the atheists and the pious, Christians and

pagans. The former had betrayed the religion of their ancestors, and were, he said, "now advancing, not so much against *us* as against those very gods whom [they] have abandoned. But the present occasion shall prove which of us is mistaken in his judgment, and shall decide between our gods and those whom our opponents profess to honor." Allowance being made for Eusebius' rewriting of the speech, no reason remains for rejecting it entirely. At the climax of a long-drawn-out contest of religions, raised through successive levels of physical violence from sporadic lynchings under Marcus Aurelius to the systematic oppression by all the powers of Diocletian's, Galerius', and Maximin Daia's governments, the final act was fittingly a battle, and the opposed convictions of Licinius and Constantine naturally assumed a physical form. Men expected this, just as, or because, they expected divine forces to express themselves in physical forms, in droughts, plagues, civil unrest, and defeats, if hostile; or if friendly, in good harvests and victories. For Constantine, Christianity was not only a way of life but a way of winning.

In February, 324, he left Sirmium for Thessalonica, organized his army, got it moving, and in June made contact with the enemy at Hadrianople. The city stands on the east bank of the Hebrus, behind which Licinius took shelter. Constantine with a feint distracted attention from the crossing-over of his main force, which proceeded to inflict a defeat and heavy casualties. Licinius rallied a part of his army at Byzantium to cover the retreat and regrouping of the rest in Asia Minor. For a while he successfully withstood a siege, until Crispus, commanding a navy, cleared the straits of hostile ships and began a blockade on the sea side. At that point Licinius promoted his Master of Offices to be Caesar, to aid in holding the straits, and himself crossed with whatever troops he could rescue, leaving Byzantium to its fate. Constantine followed, landed unopposed, and in September completed his campaign at Chrysopolis, near Chalcedon, with decisive slaughter. Licinius received special help from Gothic mercenaries, Constantine from Franks, of whom the leader Bonitus stood out. Throughout the fighting, Constantine's men, always outnumbered in one engagement after another, seem to have been led with greater enthusiasm (their emperor received a leg wound) and with greater skill. The navy, too, outmaneuvered a far more numerous foe.

From a final refuge in Nicomedia, Licinius sent Constantia to make the best terms she could for him. His Caesar was spared and exiled in southern Asia Minor, he himself was granted his life in exile at Thessalonica. A few months later, however, for reasons vague or fantastic depending on which source is followed, both Caesar and defeated Augustus were put to death. Constantine might now freely multiply his titles, as "Constantine Maximus Augustus, Conqueror," "Victor Everywhere," "Triumpher over All Peoples," and, at long last, "Ruler of the Entire Globe." The empire stood united.

VIII

CONSTANTINOPLE

The eastern half of the Mediterranean was the world of the *polis*. Here—for example, in the region that Constantine knew best, between the northern shores of the Aegean and the lower Danube—were cities such as Philippopolis, Traianopolis, Hadrianopolis, and Diocletianopolis commemorating great rulers who founded or, by extensive building and a change of name, could be said to have refounded them. Sometimes a decisive military success at or near a city provided the inspiration: for Nicopolis, "Victory-City," or Tropaeum Traiani. It fitted the role of emperor, according to this well-established custom, to signalize the defeat of Licinius by transforming Byzantium, late in 324, into Constantinopolis. Since there were no strict rules about it, he could choose this rather than Chrysopolis or any other site in the vicinity to bear the new title. Byzantium looked out over a natural crossroads and a spectacular view.

To make it the empire's capital was a different matter altogether. If Constantine meant to move about from one place to another, or if authority were to be divided on nearly equal terms among two or more rulers, several sites at once might claim the honor of being called an imperial residence and seat of government, with a court and palace but without challenge to the age and preeminence of Rome. A permanent and official center of state rather

than the traditional one, however, could not be so much as
thought of until Rome had been decisively thrust out of
mind.

A decade or so after his conversion, Constantine still
planned to be buried in the old city, or rather, just outside,
on the Via Labicana. A family mausoleum was constructed there, containing a beautiful porphyry sarcophagus, its scenes of triumph over bearded barbarians
evidently not intended for Helena, whose body later lay
there, but for her son. It is easy to guess some of the reasons why he changed his mind. Foremost was the progress
of his alienation from the nobles, which was far advanced
by the 320's. Its course was traced in a previous chapter.
So we hear, for instance, of a symptomatic and unusual
step, the condemnation of a former consul and urban
prefect. In the same period, about 324, Optatianus Porphyrius suffered exile, why or where we do not know,
though it was not for his religion. He was Christian, moreover of high lineage, and attached by friendship to a
specially influential member of the family Bassi, the consul
of 331, Junius Bassus, praetorian prefect of Italy for fourteen years. Bassus built a famous basilica on the Esquiline
hill. Its decorations were pagan, its donor the friend of a
Christian poet. Bassus' own religion cannot be guessed. He
owed his long tenure of office in Italy to his attachments
in both camps, the Roman-pagan and the imperial-Chris-
tian.

The two were driven farther apart by the celebration of
Constantine's twentieth year of rule. It began in Nicomedia
with frankly Christian festivities, coin imagery, and fan-
fare. In the course of the next six or eight months, however, he prepared for a visit to Rome (July, 326) by a
number of conciliatory gestures—held the consulate with

his son Constantius II (plate XI), advertised his entry on office *in absentia* through time-honored parade scenes of an elephant-drawn chariot under the legend, "Eternal Glory to the Senate and the Roman People"; even separately distinguished, in coins of appropriately descending weights, the senate, equestrians, and *populus*. Probably at this time or not long after, incidentally, he admitted Optatianus Porphyrius again to his favor.

But the trip to Rome in the early summer, lasting many weeks, must have reminded him of the remoteness of the capital. It was, in contrast to the reborn Byzantium, or Sirmium, a city where nothing happened, but only where things once had happened, long ago, out of reach of challenge or correction. Byzantium he could get at, to remake according to his beliefs, whereas Rome's prepotent errors were a matter of history—and that he could not change. The members of a senate a thousand years old received him coolly; so did the populace. When, for the second time, he refused homage to Jupiter on the Capitoline, some sort of riot broke out. On the religious question, if there was a middle ground of discretion and ambiguity occupied by men like Junius Bassus, there were also on both sides of it areas beyond compromise. Time must decide between them. Meanwhile the angry emperor, after only a short stay, turned from this sunset city with its ancient, irreconcilable observances, and set out for the more brilliant East.

Emotional and religious reasons for abandoning Rome were very strongly reinforced by others of a different kind. In equipoise, the Mediterranean world had once rested in Italy. Now its weight had shifted to a new center; the empire was tipping eastward. Its rulers since the turn of the second century had looked to Syria as their spiritual or original home, to Arabia, Thrace, above all, to Pannonia, Dalmatia, and Moesia, the whole middle Danube area that brought forth the Tetrarchs and the Flavian dynasty. It was eastern priests and prophets who directed men in worship and who in every province inspired the dominant cults, of Mithra, for example, or Sol, or of the ultimate victor, Christianity. If the West offered the best troops (increasingly barbarian), yet the East, its trade and markets and communications far less damaged by invasions, could and did bear more than its share of the cost of defense. The future itself, though grim enough, seemed to belong to the East. So proclaimed the oracles. All men knew them. "The Roman name," wrote Lactantius in the *Divine Institutes*, "which now controls the globe—my mind shudders to declare it, but I will say what must come to pass—will be taken away from the earth, and dominion will return to Asia. Once more the East will be master and the West its slave."

The Byzantine age had not begun, but the Roman was over. The way station to a future point of balance lay in between, stretching from the Alps to the Bosporus. To this region, Diocletian's capital at Nicomedia diffused much wealth; Maximian reared his palace at his birthplace, Sirmium, and that city, as we have seen, enjoyed the frequent patronage and presence of Constantine; Galerius magnificently adorned Thessalonica, erecting there a palace, arch, hippodrome, and mausoleum (now a church), while Serdica, near which he had been born, also prospered in his time, and by the end of Constantine's reign was quite transformed in the neighborhood of its forum. The effects that followed at Trèves from the concentration of state officials now similarly favored eastern cities. As the size of government increased in the later third and fourth centuries, and its units were multiplied by splitting the older provinces into two or three smaller ones, each with its judicial, fiscal, and military staff, more towns attained the status of capitals, and underwent a permanent expansion to make room for a mint, a state weapons factory, a dock-yard, or a law court. With these came scores of bureau-crats, spreading into the open countryside outside the walls and putting up rich houses for themselves and their fam-ilies.

In an age in which the distribution of wealth depended to an unprecedented degree on the direct presence of the state, loss of such operations meant an instant loss of reve-nue, too—as, for instance, when the imperial mints at Carthage, Lyons, and London closed up under Constan-tine, and new ones started work at Sirmium and Constanti-nople. The same sort of change could be traced in another chain of effects. Once the main link from Italy to the Aegean, the Via Egnatia, had spread commerce and wealth along its length. When the old capital surrendered a part of its primacy, the flow of traffic accordingly shifted northwards to a different path; the Via Egnatia fell into the shadows and the route Milan-Aquileia-Sirmium-Serdica emerged into the light. Not only did the chief cities on this road grow richer, but the intervening country as well. It was traversed by Diocletian in two leisurely, careful tours of inspection, and a dozen times by Constantine. Through the dates and place of issue of their laws we can sometimes follow their progress in the region, list the cities they stopped at, and identify the problems and officials from every province that sought them out on the road to gain the benefit of an imperial decision. We can imagine, upon a quiet countryside, the effect of the imperial proces-sion, so slow and lumbering yet so much the embodiment of instant, unexpected change, passing like a cyclone among scattered villages and peasants agog, and leaving among them memories of its passage good and bad, coins and corvées. Milestones from the reigns of the two emperors, attesting repairs, dot the principal routes. New posting stations were built, ruined ones renovated. Thracian farms supplying armies on the march and expanded urban markets flourished as never before, and the whole area drew in manufactures from Asia Minor, even initiating production of its own, such as silver reliefs, for northern military centers. Such was the condition of the Danube-Balkan provinces. Their fortunes rested firmly on a foundation of economic, strategic, and political realities.

Military centers performed a task essential to the wellbeing of the inward regions that they sheltered, for pressure from beyond the Danube continued to arouse anxiety throughout Constantine's later years. An important entrance into enemy territory was made in 328: the stone bridge, longest ever built by the Romans, spanning the marshes and the Danube from Oescus to Sucidava. Its significance can be read in coin reliefs: Constantine, on hand for the inauguration, is led across by Victoria toward a kneeling barbarian on the far side. Milestones tell of work on the road farther northward still, to Romula fortified by Constantine; and to the same impetus and occasion belong the ponderous battlements, resembling a medieval donjon, that form the corner of Sucidava. The line Oescus-Sucidava-Romula constituted a visible and most imposing claim to intervene in affairs beyond the river—a claim made good when in 332 the Sarmatians could no longer defend themselves against the Goths on their flanks and appealed to the Romans for help. Commanded by Constantine II, the armies were successful, inflicting casualties esti-

mated at a hundred thousand, and capturing the son of
the Gothic king. War ended in a treaty by which the van-
quished, in exchange for yearly supplies of provisions,
promised friendship, defense, and contingents of their soldiers such as had fought for Licinius. But the Goths renounced the treaty after Constantine's death.

Involvement with the Sarmatians was not over. They
turned against their benefactors; but their renewed hostility
promptly broke apart in a civil war and the losers had to
beg asylum from Constantine (334). He settled enormous
numbers of their men, women, and children in the lower
Danube region. Refugee Taifali and Vandals later received
the same treatment, the first going to Asia Minor, the second to Pannonia. It was a familiar way of handling such
peoples. Just like the Franks, these tribes farmed deserted
lands, strengthened depleted garrisons, or joined the mobile
army. At Intercisa, on the Pannonian stretch of the river,
an interesting confusion of cultures resulted from the policy of admitting aliens to the empire. Here archeology
reveals vestigial Syrian influences, from a mounted squad-
ron that had been stationed there; Burgundian, by way of
Noricum to the northeast; Vandal, from forced settlements
and army drafts; and, after Constantine, Rhenish German,
the consequence again of troop transfers; so that, by the
second half of the fourth century, the Romanized elements
had almost vanished. The intensified use that Constantine
made of barbarians in border areas and in the army, already
mentioned in regard to the western provinces, can be occasionally detected and generally presumed all along the
Danube, too. It would be hard to imagine the massive,
really uncontrolled, and fateful admission of Goths to the
empire in the 370's, had precedents on a large scale not
been established in the 330's.

Constantine's preoccupation with the safety of the lower Danube, of which he was forever reminding his subjects through Victory legends of one type or another on his coinage, produced also the type of the camp gate to advertise his care for frontier fortification (plate VIIB). He had a great deal to be proud of. Scythia provides a good illustration. It was a province split off from Moesia by Diocletian; its capital was Tomis, to which Diocletian's treasury provided a grand new town gate. Elsewhere in the province he made visits of inspection, built roads, erected forts, and stationed troops. Constantine did still more. He restored Tropaeum Traiani in a major way, "from the very foundations, . . . for the greater security of the frontier, after the tribes of barbarous races were everywhere subdued." So an inscription tells us. At Troesmis and a half-dozen nearby sites he strung castles thickly around the bend of the Danube. Histria greatly expanded its trade, put up many new public buildings, and attracted a dense population. All of Scythia enjoyed unbroken peace because of the elaborate measures for its defense. Behind the shield of forts, a marked economic revival took place. Its happy state is representative generally of Thrace, Moesia, and Pannonia in the first three or four decades of the fourth century.

It is important to note, from a more distant perspective, how wide and steady these developments were. On a relatively modest level, they improved the fortunes of particular cities or particular stretches of the border under Aurelian, or earlier still. The policy of ungrudging commitment of force to the lower Danube antedated Diocletian. His successors, including Constantine, ended in concentrating more troops in this region than could be found in any other of a similar size. Emperors, when they had the choice, made their homes in Nicomedia, Thessalonica, Sirmium or

Serdica, and delegated their Caesars to less vital posts at Antioch or Trèves, because on the lower Danube could be found the pick of the men who were the most essential to the ruler, his soldiers. Opportunities to cultivate their loyalty were best here, where the enemy most seriously threatened the empire; and from the threat could be snatched the political profit of great victories. Wherever a garrison was stationed, money abounded, too. The military chest formed the emperor's chief concern; and the chief mints and the boxes of bullion that traveled around with the court served the needs of the army's payday, diffusing wealth along the roads that joined one fort or government headquarters to another, and nourishing farms and officers' villas in the neighborhood of such centers. Small wonder, then, that Constantine, before 324, seriously thought of establishing himself at Sirmium, and then at Serdica—perhaps also at Thessalonica.* Byzantium was only the last of several candidates.

Though, in the long view, and for the clearest and best established reasons, the choice of a new capital near the Bosporus was natural, one might almost say inevitable, yet the fourth-century mind did not explain events of import without bringing in miracles. Certainly Constantine did not. The renaming of Byzantium he decided on "at God's command," as he declared to his subjects in a law of 334; and some generations afterwards, stories were in circulation that told of a divine vision directing him to the spot, or of an angel unseen by others who led him on the circuit of the new walls. The wizard-philosopher Sopater was said to have assisted in the ceremonies of dedication; and pagans

---

*By the fifth century, legend added Troy to the list of capitals he considered.

believed that Constantinople as a New Rome, after the old
had run its appointed course of years, somehow insured a
second lease of life to the empire according to the prescrip-
tion of an oracle.

The birthday of Constantinople fell on May 11, 330.
Festivities lasted forty days. Most of them took place in a
new, marble-paved, oval forum, surrounded by a two-
story marble portico, in the middle of which stood a porphyry column bearing a gilt statue of the emperor. It held
on its right hand the orb of world power. Inside the orb
was a piece of the True Cross. From the forum eastwards
Constantine had lined the main avenue with more porticoes
(the Royal) on each side, containing scores and scores of
statues. It ran past a new basilica as meeting place for the
senate, and so to the new palace, one side of which presented an elaborate window or gallery opening, as the imperial box, on the Hippodrome. On the closing day of the
ceremonies a parade of soldiers in dress uniform, bearing
white candles and escorting a golden statue of the Fortune
of Constantinople on a wagon, moved through crowds
and acclamations along the avenue to the Hippodrome, cir-
cled it, and stopped before the imperial box. Constantine
rose from his seat to hail the image, commanded it to be
placed with a matching Tyche of Rome in a new chapel,
and arranged for the same parade to be held on the same
day each year thereafter. Festivities ended with horse
races, and publication of coin reliefs depicting Constantinople with a ship, as queen of the seas, or with wolf and
twins, as Second Rome.

The monuments involved in the parade—forum, porticoes, and the rest—were all the creations of Constantine
de novo, or, like the Hippodrome, major renovations or
enlargements of previous construction; nor do those so far

mentioned by any means complete the list in the city. Two other lengths of porticoes framed the tip of the peninsula on its north and south sides, another led out to the main gate on the west. The Milion, or golden milestone, from which all distances were measured, had an elaborate tetra-style cupola over it; the senate had a second meeting place fronting on a pillared piazza, the Augusteum. Besides special palace baths, a splendidly expanded public baths building opened its doors to the populace, and learned men received accommodations to their taste in the Capitolium and the Octagon, an embryonic university.

We need not attempt a full catalogue of the emperor's achievements in construction, but they were both grand and numerous. Particularly striking was the speed with which they transformed a city that had just stood a siege. For this, a price had to be paid, in structures poorly put together, like the palace, or soon requiring repair, or begun ambitiously but not finished until much later; and throughout were signs of pillage. In the forum, the por-phyry column came from Rome, the statue atop from Ilion (it was once a figure of Apollo, the head recut). For the Hippodrome, Delphi willy-nilly contributed a colossal tripod dedicated to the oracle by the triumphant Greek confederates in 478 B.C., and other Greek cities were robbed of other works in sculptured bronze. Miles of porticoes, their lower stories promptly filled by silversmiths along one avenue, shops along a second, public scribes and law-yers along a third, displayed in their upper arcades endless lines of stolen statuary from all over the East, some of a secular nature, some formerly cult images. Rome's treas-ures alone were safe. The emperor had there set up a curator of public art and decreed penalties for the theft of marble columns.

In 324 the city's landward, western gate had stood where Constantine's forum was shortly to emerge. Beyond stretched perhaps a few streets of suburbs. Constantine had bigger ideas. He moved the walls a mile and a half farther to the west, turning the whole great tongue of land into almost an island city, to which his son was to add seawalls later. He more than quadrupled the urban area.

Who was to build here? A range of enticements and punishments worked together to draw in an adequate labor force for the necessary housing. Skilled workmen came from as far away as Naples. The difficulties were extreme. We may recall the need for artisans drawn from Britain to aid in the expansion and adornment of Autun, or laws of the 330's frankly confessing the ubiquitous lack of architects, plasterers, mosaicists, cabinetmakers, masons, gilders, smiths, marble workers, glaziers, and a host of others detailed in a desperate list, to whom, as encouragement, the state extended exemption from *munera* and rewards for undergoing apprenticeships. All these crafts had languished, in default of settled times, general prosperity, patronage, and customers. In an instant, they were to be revived for the supreme patron, the emperor.

But who was to live here, once the houses and public squares were built? Again the government used both the stick and carrot to fill the empty blocks. As to the carrot: The attraction above all that brought in new citizens was the presence of the emperor, and with him a praetorian prefect, Masters of Infantry and Cavalry, two treasury counts, the chancery, thousands of lesser officials, and, indirectly, still more thousands of litigants, scribes, and lawyers clustering around a dozen courts of appeal. Constantinople moreover had its own, and more than munici-

PLATE I Head of Constantine, once in his basilica, now in the Museo dei Conservatori.

PLATE II *(Below)* Re-shaping the emperor's image. One stereotype prevails for the Tetrarchs, Diocletian (A), Licinius (B), Constantius (C) — even for Constantine, before the mints got used to him (D from Rome, 306-307; E from Siscia, 315-316). In 326 appears the diadem (F), and his double chin about the same time (G).

PLATE III *(Facing Page)* A third-century mosaic from the mausoleum of the Julii under St. Peter's, showing Christ-Sol, radiate, on a chariot. Below, to the left, is Invictus Constantinus on a coin of 313, with Sol's chariot on his shield and Sol's radiate profile behind him. To the right is the more famous coin of the same year, with a tiny Chi-Rho on the helmet and Rome's wolf and twins on the shield.

PLATE IV The Milvian bridge.

PLATE V (*Above*) The Arch of Constantine.

PLATE VI (*Opposite, top*) The basilica at Trèves.

PLATE VII (*Opposite, bottom*) A model of the fortress at Deutz; below, a coin advertises military building through the Providentia of the Caesars, with their statues over the camp gate.

PLATE VIII The summer palace on the Moselle, near Trèves.

pal, senate. It was recruited by the emperor in part afresh, in part from among senators of Rome. For any that would move to the new capital he provided a grand residence, and whoever of lower rank built a house for himself thereby qualified for free food handouts. Lastly, a law was passed requiring anyone in Asia Minor in possession of crown lands (which enjoyed a desirable tax status) to build a second residence in Constantinople.

The emperor improved the water supply by means of a new aqueduct, and granted exemption from *munera* to property owners abutting it, in return for their labor to keep it in good repair. The same exemption, in whatever town they inhabited, rewarded shipowners who enrolled in the supplying of the new dole to Constantinople, and they were assured of additional payments on their cargoes. The system got under way in 332. It brought grain from Egypt sufficient to feed a list of eighty thousand persons. The total population was double that figure, perhaps more, and of course went on growing dramatically over the next hundred years. The initial impetus, however, was Constantine's, and made a deep impression on his near contemporaries. Two pagans of the next generation respectively attribute to Constantine the emptying of the treasury, and the emptying of "the other cities," in the course of his attempts truly to refound Byzantium. Though the bias of the writers turns their evaluation into an attack, it is clear that, for good or ill, a most extraordinary and successful experiment in urban development was going on in the late 320's and the 330's, backed up by resourceful and imperious application of government powers. It terminated an eastward trend of more than a century, anchored it for good at the meeting point of Europe and Asia, and confirmed, as it was itself suggested by, the prosperity of Thrace and neighboring provinces, through which it radiated vital energies.

Constantinople did not escape the mark of its builder. Others before him had established the role—Diocletian at Nicomedia, Galerius at Thessalonica. But Constantine made it Christian. To the traditional palace, porticoes, and racecourse he added churches; and the plan and construction of them introduced the Roman model to the East. The church of Holy Peace was barely finished, and of Holy Wisdom barely begun, before his death. The Church of the Apostles, however, he did complete, on the former site of a temple to Aphrodite. A martyrium of basilical form led, not to an apse, but to a rotunda around which stood memorials of the Twelve; in their midst, the sarcophagus to hold the emperor. Eusebius lingers lovingly on the rich marbles, gilding, carving, and elaborate plan of the whole complex.

The displacement of Aphrodite symbolized a wider policy. In the new capital the old gods had no place. Aside from two or three shrines without cult, sheltering abstractions like the city's Tyche, temples disappeared, and images were recut to inoffensive forms, or emerged into the unkind light of day as ornament for some public arcade. What henceforth preserved the city was not Jupiter but the benign presence of the True Cross, the Rod of Moses, or other holy relics. Constantinople, personified, in coin reliefs held a cross surmounted by a globe.

And yet the imagery surrounding her on other occasions simply repeated the attributes of the older capital, as bringer of victory, bestower of peace, source of abundance. Her seven hills by mere designation conformed more to those on the Tiber than to actual topography; her fourteen administrative boroughs matched those of Rome. The new capital had its Golden Milestone, its forum; it had its senate, perfectly useless, perfectly artificial, indeed nothing but a social rank, above which the emperor placed the ancient distinction of the "patriciate" exhumed from the vaults of Roman history. The people must receive their bread dole, like the *populus Romanus;* but quite extraordinarily, advertisement of the now duplicated largesses appears on the city's coins *in Latin,* for the benefit of citizens who, as a contemporary maliciously notes, could not even pronounce the emperor's name properly. In so many respects did Constantinople aspire to be, in the words of her founder, or of the poet Optatianus Porphyrius, *altera Roma,* "a second Rome."

Veneration for the past prevented a more arrogant challenge to Rome. The title "New Rome" only came into use for Constantinople long after Constantine's death. Constantinopolitan senators yielded in rank to Roman, and the city's magistracies were different and fewer. For a while, in fact, Constantine's ambition for Constantinople seems not to have extended beyond the original narrow walls of Byzantium. His visit to Rome in 326 changed things. It was after his return that the great expansion of the area of the city took place; and, with that, he committed himself to making Constantinople a second and rising capital.

The old he did not touch. None of its privileges suffered diminution; its people continued to receive a dole, even elaborated to include a greater variety of articles as time went on; its port at Ostia remained busy, though less so than in the days of Marcus Aurelius; its rich men still moved from one high office to another, though jostled increasingly by upstart army and Eastern careerists, and still could keep up their gifts of shows in the amphitheatre.

They still controlled the bestowal of priesthoods by recommendation to the pontifex maximus, the emperor. Only, the official head of paganism was now a Christian—*o tempora!*—and the actual center of the Roman world, after a thousand years, was now removed from the historic by a thousand miles.

IX

NICAEA

One of the shaping influences most easily followed and most important through Constantine's career is that of government power. He made no contribution to absolute monarchy. He inherited it from a long line of predecessors on the throne. But it *was* absolute, and one searches vainly in the sources for any hint of limitation on the theory of it. Practice, to be sure, differed. Despite the expansion of government over the preceding generation and the further measures that Constantine took, many areas of life eluded his reach; but he possessed an untrammeled right to say what he wanted done, and a formidable range of authorities and instruments to impose his will on his empire.

When he turned to the expression of his religious beliefs through his official position, his first acts, though prompt and energetic, nevertheless wholly lacked imagination. That quality could better be found in the programs of Maximin Daia, earlier, or of Julian, later. Obedient to the most ancient and obvious customs of benefaction, Constantine relied on mere quantity, he merely built big—in Trèves or Cirta, but especially in Rome and Constantinople. His war on temples, which in any event he did not press forward until the 330's, recapitulated the persecutions; his restoration to the Church of confiscated property simply reversed them. It never occurred to him, nor, of course, to a great many ecclesiastical leaders, to wonder whether wealth, grandeur, honorific titles, endowments, silver candelabras, marble and mosaics grew naturally out of the inwardness and previous history of Christianity. Inwardness was something on which he never wasted much time.

A decade after his conversion he was still personally decreeing crucifixion as a punishment. The right of parents to expose unwanted children to die he never attacked, despite opposite views which he might have read in the *Divine Institutes;* and there, too, Lactantius had harshly condemned gladiatorial spectacles as "public murders," which, notwithstanding, the emperor left untouched until 325. We will return to the spirit of Constantine's legislation, but the contrast is clear between his attention to the outward parts and appearance of the Church, and on the other hand his inattention to its spiritual meaning.

In dealing with the Church in Africa, his favor was characteristically directed to the official structure. Orthodox priests were to enjoy certain valuable immunities. Throughout the empire, those who were celibate and women who had taken vows of chastity were released in 320 from long-established disabilities which had been originally intended as encouragements to larger families. Certain monks and nuns received individual grants of food from public storehouses. Clerical exemption from municipal *munera* was extended into Italy; and in 316, in a law addressed to Ossius (perhaps because inspired by him), slave-owners received permission to free their slaves not only before secular officials but through a far less complicated attestation in the presence of a bishop. Episcopal courts were soon authorized to hear any civil case, by change of venue from other courts and without right of further appeal. They became, that is, courts of last instance.

The pope Silvester obliged clergy to bring their cases only before bishops. Finally, in 321, Sunday was declared an official holiday, and bequests to the Church were brought within the protection of the law.

These measures, all prior to Constantine's second war with Licinius, made his religious bias perfectly explicit. So, too, did his promotion of his coreligionists. Although to the day of his death he still made appointments from among pagans, according to merit or political considerations, yet his immediate entourage betrayed his partiality. His was a predominantly Christian court, it was slowly but visibly becoming a Christian empire, and proof lay in the privileges showered on the Church; hence a law of 329, restricting rights to join the clergy. Holy orders had become a refuge from burdensome taxes and municipal duties. Before the reign was over, pagans and Christians alike could discern, with pretended or genuine distress, the contamination of the Church by persons converted only on the surface, or for the wrong reasons.

Conquest of the East opened up a new field for reformation. All Licinius' hateful measures must be undone: exemptions, privileges, property, rank, and exiles restored; convicts released from state factories, mines, quarries, and jails; and the enslaved made free. Some of the crown lands now coming into Constantine's possession he promptly reassigned as further endowments to St. Paul's, St. Peter's, and to other Roman basilicas; a program of church building in the Holy Land got under way (below, pp. 188–90). He could not raise the dead, but what government could do in the wake of the persecutions, that he did happily. He was in an exultant mood. For his eastern provinces, in a public letter, he reviewed the changes wrought by his recent victory.

Such was the weight of impiety thus burdening the human scene; and society, in danger of utter destruction as if from some pestilential disease, stood in need of a great and saving care. What alleviation did the Divinity purpose? What release from this dreadful situation? One must surely consider it the Divinity that truly is, and throughout time holds the fullness of power; so there can certainly be no presumption in employing eloquence to acknowledge the Almighty's grace. For He sought me as a fitting instrument of his will, and judged me worthy; and, setting out from that ocean around Britain and the regions where by some necessity the sun sinks, I repelled and scattered every evil with the aid of a greater power, to the end that at the same time the whole human race might be recalled to the veneration of the most holy law through the instruction afforded by my role as agent.

The note of mission sounds in this passage with even more emphatic confidence than a few years earlier, when he spoke to the erring Donatists.

He now became acquainted with Eusebius, bishop of Caesarea in Palestine; and through Eusebius' *On the Life of Constantine* (not meant to be an ordinary biography but rather an essay dealing with the emperor's religious side) we in turn get our first intimate picture of Constantine. It is more a montage than a photograph. Many elements in it do not fit together chronologically. The artist who assembled it paid little attention to dates. Perhaps they do not matter very much. At any rate, at some point after 324, the emperor's residence had become like a church, entered under a vivid allegorical painting that showed what one might expect to find within: piety at war with evil; and to the great audience hall the members of the palace staff and sizeable crowds from the city used to gather in answer to an imperial summons, to hear sermons which, with reading, prayer, instruction, and laborious devotion, the emperor had worked on often far into the night, and which he delivered with the utmost earnestness. Like George II of England at the premiere of the *Messiah*, Constantine would acknowledge the more uplifting parts of his own discourse by rising from his throne. He was not too proud to do as much for someone else. As Eusebius once embarked on a speech about the Holy Sepulcher, the emperor stood up. The speech went on and on; but the speaker, anxious not to incommode his audience, at last faltered. Would his majesty be pleased to sit down? By no means. Might the speaker bring his thoughts to a close? Certainly not. The subject deserved a copious treatment. Thus Eusebius was obliged to continue.

There were smaller assemblies that Constantine used for the discussion of religious topics. Pagan officials might be the object of remarks aimed toward their conversion; pagan philosophers might be discountenanced, if they knew what was good for them, by the force of the emperor's reasoning. To Acesius, leader of a sect of extreme rigorists who taught that those who had surrendered to the terror of the persecutions could never be readmitted to communion, Constantine replied, "Set up a ladder, Acesius, and mount to heaven alone." Every Sunday, divine services were said. The court was urged to attend. The emperor himself prayed daily in his private apartments or in a chapel tent that followed him about. On campaign once, and spear in hand, he happened to encounter a courtier whom he believed guilty of more than the usual extortions. "How far," he said to him, "will our insatiability extend?" And then with the point of the spear he marked out on the ground that little box of earth that, after death, we can alone call our own.

He encouraged Christianity in the army, without any sudden success. Sunday was marked off for rest and worship, and for the recitation of a prayer in Latin personally composed by the emperor. "We know Thou art God alone; we recognize in Thee our king. We call on Thee for aid. From Thee we receive victory, through Thee we are made greater than our enemies. We recognize Thy grace in present blessings and hope on Thee for the future. We all beseech Thee, we implore Thee to preserve our king Constantine and his pious sons safe and victorious to the end of our days"—very much a soldier's prayer, and one that a pagan could recite without heartburning, especially on the appointed Sun-day, *dies Solis.*

A civilian audience, particularly in the eastern provinces, could safely be addressed in a less ambiguous fashion. In the city where he lodged, Nicomedia and then Constantinople, he ordered Easter to be celebrated publicly, and on the night before, the streets were lit throughout with candles and torches. This was clear enough Christianity. Moreover, shortly after his defeat of Licinius he circulated two general letters aimed respectively at believers and nonbelievers, emphasizing the equation, piety equals victory, true worship brings its rewards on earth, and (just the point on which Lactantius insisted at such length, in his account of *The Deaths of the Persecutors*) God's enemies and the enemies of His servants had in the past suffered, as they would certainly in the future suffer, a hideous fate. These views, to the same audience, Constantine repeated once again, concluding,

I desire Thy people to live in peace, undivided, for the sake of our common world and the good of all men. Let those who still delight in error participate in peace and tranquillity to the same degree as those who believe. For the revival in fellowship is for all, and may suffice to lead them into the straight path. Let no one disturb anyone else, let each do as his spirit bids him. Those wiser ones should believe that they alone will live holily and purely whom God calls to stand on His holy laws, while those who are withdrawn therefrom possess as they please their temples of error. We for our part have the most glorious house of Thy truth, given us as a natural possession. For the others, however, we pray that they too may gain joy through common concord (*homonoia*).

The word, or its Latin equivalent, has been encountered in Constantine's handling of the Donatist dispute, and recurs again and again and again in his addresses to the Church of the East. It is the key to his whole Church policy. It underlies one decision after another—and one synonym after another, too: "fellowship," "fraternity," "harmony," and so forth.

Concord by any name was notably lacking in the realm to which he fell heir in 324. Part of the trouble arose from the schism that stood for severity, Meletianism; part, by far the most important, arose from quite a different dispute about the nature of the Trinity. The history of Arianism returns us to the period of Licinius' rule; and its setting requires the mention of some well-known and obvious, but essential, facts.

The East, as was said, was the world of the *polis*. But that meant more than a relatively high level of urbanization. It meant a contentious independence of one city from another, and memories of an age when each had asserted its special claims and strength against all its neighbors through war. If actual fighting had long ceased, challenge took a sublimated form in boasts of wealth, size, beauty, derivation, or founding; and, increasingly, the Christian community had crystallized out of paganism around the bishops and churches of these individual cities. Here was no Rome, no natural leader or arbiter. The alternative, large councils, was in its infancy. Besides, as a second major difference distinguishing it from the West, the eastern Church had a rich heritage of philosophy, developed likewise in contention, sharpened in centuries of debate, apt for application to the problems of theological interpretation. When we look specifically at creeds, though we find in the East as in the West the same broad terms of understanding, yet dozens or scores of cities had each their own versions, and minor differences were pressed with much greater acuity and logical penetration. Prideful diversity and too much cleverness were the father and mother of heresy.

When the theologian Lucian died in the persecutions, he left behind him a number of former pupils, including Eusebius, bishop of Nicomedia,* Arius, presbyter of Alexandria, and other heads of the communities at Nicaea, Chalcedon, and elsewhere. They shared an intellectual arrogance, they shared the bond of their training, and they shared roughly similar theological views. Apparently all inclined to see in God a perfect being from whom nothing was lacking whatsoever, complete in Himself. By radical extension, this could lead to the denial that Father and Son participated in a common divinity, and to the assertion that God, being

---

*The two Eusebii are cumbersome to distinguish. The name alone will mean the bishop of Caesarea, in these pages, and the other Eusebius will be identified by his city.

all, had not only created Christ at some specific though
unknown time, but, further, had created Him out of nothing, to be no more than His Demiurge or fashioning
instrument in the material world. These shocking ideas
emerged gradually from the teachings of Arius.

Of blameless life and imposing dignity, an ascetic and a
skillful dialectician, Arius stood high in the opinion of his
bishop, Alexander. But he could not be left uncorrected.
Nearly a hundred Egyptian and Libyan bishops, being
called together in about 318 to consider the case, backed
up the previous findings of Alexandrian hearings. Arius
was condemned as a heretic and excommunicated. The
story did not end there. What he taught had become the
talk of the town. Everyone chose sides on the matter,
and partisan jingles were sung in the streets. Meanwhile, the
cause of the controversy had gone off to Caesarea, where
Eusebius received him cordially and wrote to two friends
(among others), the bishops of Laodicea and Tyre, on
his guest's behalf. Arius next moved on to Bithynia, where
he again met with a warm welcome. Eusebius of Nicomedia was by marriage connected to the royal house, his
seat was also the eastern capital, and Licinius and Constantia
showed him great favor. He in his province and Eusebius
in Palestine summoned synods which vindicated Arius and
restored him to his rank and duties in Alexandria. Alexander angrily rejected the intrusion into his see and re-
doubled his efforts to rally outside strength, writing to
his friend Eustathius, and to no less than seventy other
dignitaries of the eastern Church from whom he might
hope for support. Two of these letters survive, flinging
about various charges of self-seeking, ambition, malevo-
lence, intrigue, greed, and blasphemy.

By this time Alexander had been joined by the Meletians,

Alexandria's theaters rang with the jeers of pagans, and
nuisance suits by one party or another were springing up
like mushrooms in the civil courts. It was Carthage all
over again, but with the difference that Donatism had been
a schism focused on procedure, not on fundamental belief,
while Arianism was heresy. Whatever its nature, however—
and Constantine was at first ill informed about it—he
determined to end it if he could. He sent off Ossius, his
reverend Spanish adviser, to investigate on the spot, to
deliver a letter to the disputants, and to make peace between them (November, 324). Ossius promptly allied himself with Alexander and with another presbyter destined to
carry the struggle forward for decades on his own shoulders alone, Athanasius. In the long run, however, Ossius
may not have helped the claims of imperial arbitration by
his partisanship, and the letter he bore certainly struck the
wrong note. Contrasting *homonoia*, predictably, with the
sorry state to which discord had reduced Africa, and ending with yet another appeal to the same desired concord, in
the body of the letter Constantine reproached both Arius
and Alexander for their mere love of argument. Hardly
tactful. Worse yet, he found its cause "perfectly inconsequential and quite unworthy of such contentious debate
. . . extremely minor and highly inconsequential, . . .
suggested by unprofitable leisure. . . . [The differences
are] minor and extremely trifling, . . . few and idle disputes about words," and so on. Indeed, he sought to con-
vince them that they were really at one on the fundamentals,
despite superficial and apparent disagreement. If not that,
then all their assertions and counterassertions about the
nature of Christ should never have been thrown open to
argument, since to do so had now as always shaken the
faith of simple believers by unanswerable riddles, impious

curiosity, and the probing of questions which, the emperor hints, even the disputants themselves did not fully understand.

It is clear that Constantine, for one, did not understand them. He was quite beyond his depth. What he felt comfortable with was Latin Christianity, and the kind of reassurance he could find in Lactantius: that basic doctrine explained itself, that the very masters of sophistry admitted as much; whereas their unrestrained conjectures had led only to confusion. What of the Greek tradition of rational inquiry? All vain. "Better," Constantine advised an assembly of bishops in the previous year,

better to address ourselves to the objects within our powers and within the reach of our nature, for what persuades us in the course of a debate distracts most of us from the truth of reality, as has befallen many philosophers who exercise their wits on reasons and the investigation of the essence of things. And whenever the magnitude of the question outstrips their inquiry, they bury the truth in methodological differences. They end up teaching conflicting opinions, and attack each other's positions, even the men who lay claim to wisdom. Hence, factious divisions among the common people, too.

He expresses the point of view of a practical man, perhaps an impatient one, certainly not a speculative one. And it fitted a person with vast responsibilities. He had the care of sixty or eighty million bodies whose well-being he was convinced depended on a tribute of worship to the Christian God. Everything in his life over the preceding dozen years reinforced his conviction. To prolong the blessings that flowed from God into his reign and primacy, and so to the empire as a whole, he must assure that same tribute. Hairsplitting and argument for argument's sake divided the Church, turned men from God, and jeopardized the safety of the realm.

Already a kind of civil war infected Alexandria. It spread northward into Palestine, Syria, and Asia Minor. A synod at Antioch apparently at this time elected Eustathius bishop (early 325) only after much unseemly jockeying and lobbying. Ossius, presiding (as he had done at an earlier Alexandrian synod), added to the agenda the consideration of doctrinal questions. He won a vote for an uncompromisingly anti-Arian declaration of faith, and thus transformed the meeting into one more battle of a lengthening war. Eusebius would not sign the declaration, but appeal was promised him through a synod called at Ancyra, clearly marked for continued strife and very likely to undo the work of Antioch, since the bishop of Ancyra was a powerful Arian. It was not easy to see where matters would end.

So Ossius reported to his master in the early weeks of the year. There was no more talk of its all being inconsequential. Instead, Constantine resolved to draw in the entire empire to a single concerted effort at reunification. The decision once taken, messengers galloped out from the capital along the public postal routes, picking up fresh mounts at every station and spreading the summons west to Spain, eastward to the lands of the Tigris and Euphrates. The invitations urged haste; envoys had at their disposal public conveyances; by the opening session on June 19, 325, close to three hundred gathered at the city named Victory, Nicaea. They came from faraway Arabia, Persia, Scythia; an overwhelming majority from the nearer eastern provinces, with especially large delegations from Egypt; even a sprinkling from the West, where no one had the least interest in the controversy—not Silvester of Rome, then,

who pleaded his age and infirmities, but two of his presbyters, and Caecilian of Carthage, and two or three more. If
token representation counted, Nicaea was ecumenical, and
the first such council in history.

The growth of Arianism has a certain drama to it. The
story opens on a tall, thin, serious youth traveling from
Libya to Antioch. There he sits on a bench with other
students in the house of Lucian, there he draws in the rich
mixture of Greek philosophy and Scripture, ponders it
alone, and argues it out with his fellows. Years later he
approaches the center of the stage again as a priest in Egypt,
though affecting the characteristic costume of the early
monks. This time others sit before him, while he teaches,
in the parish church of Baucalis. Ideas as words form rings
and eddies spreading outwards in the minds of his hearers,
engaging other loyalties, changing into actions, and the actions into patterns called "the Church of Alexandria,"
"Synod of all Egypt and Libya," or the like; radiating
further still, to touch the currents of correspondence,
friendship, or rivalry that join the great episcopal sees of the
eastern provinces; and at last taking shape in a series of
assemblies—at which point, from other directions, other
forms of action impinge, their story drawing us back
through Constantine, back to Carthage, and as far as the
Milvian Bridge.

For so historic an event, the Nicene Council remains
surprisingly obscure. But of course it represented a determined effort by a most determined man to bury differences,
and in the process he inevitably buried much else besides.
What escaped oblivion, memory bent to partisan purposes.
Only the preliminaries emerge clearly. The bishops, ranged
according to rank in two rows facing each other, met in
the main audience hall of the palace. At a sign, they rose;

three members of the royal family (but no guards) entered, and after them the emperor, gorgeously appareled
in purple, gold, and jewels. He walked through the silence
to the head of the hall and signaled for the bishops to be
seated. They indicated that he should be seated first. The
impasse was breached by everybody sitting down simultaneously, Constantine not on a raised throne but on a
modest golden chair. One of the bishops on his right in the
position of honor—whether Eusebius or Eustathius is uncertain—rose to deliver a speech of welcome to which
Constantine replied briefly in Latin, with consecutive trans-
lation, expressing his thanks to God for the present occasion, praying that the Devil might not join their
deliberations, and urging on all a spirit of peace and harmony. After that, debate commenced.

Though several persons, including Ossius, had been appointed to preside, in fact Constantine himself attended
the sessions regularly—some two months of them—and
bore the chief burden of controlling them. He knew enough
Greek to intervene effectively, and gave his opinion or
called on speakers enough to get the business of the confer-
ence done without opening the door to all the angers and
accusations that waited to come in. Considering the problems, he achieved remarkable success.

In the first place, he had to deal not with a uniform group
but a collection of individuals. Among them were some
of Christianity's heroes—Paphnutius, whose blinded eye
socket he kissed in veneration, James of Antioch, whose
piety could raise the dead, Paul of Neocaesarea with his
burned hands, all glorious and reverend survivors of the
persecutions; with them, the backbenchers, forming the
great majority of the council and representing the average-
sized and smaller sees—towns of ten or twenty thousand,

some quite isolated, their bishops resistant to change and hard put really to understand much of the discussion; finally, a dozen men from the major centers, redoubtable theologians, politicians, and administrators. Before proceedings even began, these latter had been at work. Constantine had come to some tentative agreement on the issues with Eusebius of Nicomedia, as Ossius had done with Alexander of Alexandria. Previous synods had gone over the same ground earlier still, as had numberless less formal meetings within the various parties. Nicaea thus brought to a focus well-exercised, carefully developed, intellectual positions.

And, we must add, in the second place, political positions. Though most churchmen looked on politics as only the means to an end, for some it was the end itself. The Council of Arles (314) in two of its canons forbade them to shift from one see to another; Nicaea repeated the ban; so did Serdica (343), and other councils later. What this legislation vainly tried to prevent was the upward zigzagging of ambitious persons from little communities to big, a course of advancement made easy by the natural tendency of Antioch, let us say, to offer its episcopal throne to someone of established prominence and ability at the lesser level of Caesarea (Eusebius) or Beroea (Eustathius). As Alexander put it, "Love of office and love of money are forever leading certain rogues to plot and plan for more glorious-seeming dioceses"—aided by a second, parasite type that Constantine denounced after watching the Council of Nicaea at work: "Some freely offer their allegiance for their keep, others are wont to fawn on those who control patronage."

And in the third place, intrigue was sharpened by exaggerated invective and slander habitual in Greek party politics. It crackled and burned through all serious disputes. We may just instance Constantine's description of Arius as "that shameless servant of the Devil," or the theology of Eusebius of Nicomedia as "drunken railing." Such highly colored language seems to grow more common, almost automatic, as time goes on.

Whether or not it was "drunken railing," Eusebius of Nicomedia, on behalf of Arianism, got the council off to a start with a statement of his beliefs on the Trinity. Amidst shouts of outrage, the document was literally torn to pieces. The other Eusebius, balked of his hearing at the now-canceled synod of Ancyra, and under threat of excommunication by the synod of Antioch, advanced next to offer another credo. It was the traditional one of Caesarea, along lines widely popular in Palestine and Syria. It received lengthy, at times heated, consideration. Constantine, for his part, heartily approved of it. To an emended draft, he would just like to insert, he said, the one word "consubstantial" (*homoousios*), to indicate the relation of Son to Father. Only seventeen bishops found the resultant unacceptable, and the threat of excommunication reduced this number to two, of whom Arius was one. Everyone else subscribed to what, after many vicissitudes, became the basis of later belief.

We believe in one God, maker of all things visible and invisible, and in one Lord Jesus Christ, the Son of God, only-begotten of the Father, that is, of the substance of the Father, God from God, Light from Light, true God from true God, begotten not made, consubstantial with the Father, through whom all things have come to be, both things in the heavens and on earth; who on account of us men and our salvation came down and was made flesh, became man, suffered, and rose again on the third day, ascended to the heavens, and will come to judge the living and the dead; and in the Holy Spirit. But those who say there was a time when He did not exist, and He did not exist before He was begotten, and that He came into being from nothing, or who declare that the Son of God is of another hypostasis or substance, or is created or changeable, these the Catholic Church anathematizes.

The Nicene Creed bore the imprint of controversy in the emphasis it placed on the questions that had led to the convening of the council in the first place. Earlier, and in the West, creeds were more descriptive of what Christ had done than analytical of what He was; and of course the anathemas were an innovation. "Consubstantial" was not quite new, but decidedly unfamiliar, apparently meant to expose and embarrass Arianists. With varying degrees of reluctance and inner reservation, however, all of them, even the two Eusebii, submitted to the majority plus the emperor—an overwhelming alliance. Arius went into exile (if it may be called that—at Nicomedia!) and the chief Arian writings were ordered to be surrendered on pain of death, and burned.

Next came two other problems: Meletianism and the date of Easter. Constantine personally pressed for reform of the latter, which some churches celebrated on the same day as the Jewish Passover. The emperor's passionate anti-Semitism would not suffer this, and a date already in use in Egypt and elsewhere was agreed on by all. As for the Meletians, their treatment was shaped by the lessons learned in a dozen unsuccessful years of strife with Donatism. Meletius was permitted to retain the title of bishop without real power, in his original see. His followers in the lower positions of presbyter and deacon might, by a somewhat complicated set of rules, be slowly absorbed into the hierarchy of other churches in the province. The council, with the publication of these and twenty other canons on lesser questions, now terminated.

Toward the end of its sessions, Constantine had invited it to a celebration in honor of God and *homonoia*, though the occasion coincided also with the ceremonies that opened his twentieth year of rule. While the towns and cities all held festivals and offered vows for his continued prosperity, the bishops gathered at night for a state banquet. They passed through files of the imperial guard (and what memories must those naked swords have revived in their minds) to inner apartments, where the emperor welcomed them and placed them at their dining couches, some apart, some with himself (though it is difficult to imagine Constantine taking anything lying down, even his supper). At the end of the banquet, so remarkable an act of condescension, he distributed presents to every guest. The scene fits the one, reported without context, in which Eusebius heard him describe himself as "also a bishop, and appointed by God over those outside the Church." Constantine must have meant pagans and the secular world in general, but the conception has given rise to much scholarly debate.

When one stops to think of it, his position vis-à-vis the Church was most peculiar. Unlearned in Scripture, unbaptized, without any pretense to ecclesiastical office, he embodied at the same time those secular powers which had for centuries shown to Christians only their cruel side. Who was he, then, to dictate doctrine to Christians of Africa or play host and arbiter to those of the whole East? Whatever part Ossius may have taken in the background, it was Constantine in the foreground who claimed to have first conceived the idea of an ecumenical council "according to God's suggestion" and in the capacity of "fellow servant" of the bishops to whom he sent his invitations. It was as imperial emissary, not as bishop of Cordova, that Ossius had presided over synods. The same was true of Constantine's counts presiding in later synods; and the results of ecclesiastical congresses were announced and their decisions, sometimes by exile or excommunication, were enforced by the emperor. This is why we find one synod, in 330, forbidding individual bishops to initiate appeal of any Church matters to the emperor.

People often resorted to analogies to make the subject clearer—for example, analogies between Christ and the emperor. One admirer of Constantine wrote that Christ "combats spiritual evils, you have conquered the terrestrial." Compare Eusebius' picture of the destructive demons abroad, full of hate; "but he [Constantine] like his Savior, knowing only how to save, has saved the very godless themselves, instructing them in piety." And he refers to Constantine also as a sort of bishop of bishops, or a holy prophet—often as a new Moses. The truth was that the Church had never before faced the possibility of a Christian on the throne, and the 320's and 330's were the period in which the implications of this unexpected reality had first to be thought through.

Occasion offered repeatedly in the dozen years after Nicaea. The council had spoken out, not very harshly, against a rigorist sect led by Acesius (above, p. 163) and secular legislation was needed to put its decisions into effect. The same year (326) brought the reminder that exemptions to clergy did not apply to heretics, and a letter specifically to Egypt drove the point home. Meanwhile, intransigent Arianists there had been summoned north to separate them from their audience; and Eusebius of Nicomedia, who housed them and plotted with them, so it was said, was expelled from his see by the emperor (late 325).

At this point the Procrustean concord of Nicaea dissolves
into obscurities, tergiversations, and unedifying feuds. Ossius disappears from the picture. Presumably he accompanied the emperor to Rome for the twenty-year festival, and
went on from there to retirement at Cordova. Controversy
and attack settle on the two friends, Athanasius and Eustathius, whom his absence had deprived of a spokesman at
court. Both had enemies to spare. Athanasius had played a
prominent part at Nicaea, thus directing on himself the
hostile gaze of the Arianists, and when he succeeded Alexander as bishop of Alexandria (328) they were ready for
him with accusations that he had obtained his election by
force and was denying the Meletians what Nicaea had
promised them. Further charges developed subsequently.
In 332 he had personally to rebut them in the emperor's
court, to which he had been hailed. There, for the moment,
we may leave him.

Eustathius, bishop of Antioch, fell victim to more complicated plots, of which, however, the essential condition
was the emperor's change of mind. Having dragooned his
fellow Christians into acceptance of a compromise, made
possible by a good deal of pressure and that key novelty—
or ambiguity—the term "consubstantial," Constantine
now turned about and offered reconciliation to the very
men he had opposed. His reasons are unknown. The Nicene
council, however, had been summoned too quickly—that
much became clear—before the duties of reorganizing half
of the Roman Empire, and his own rather resistant intellect,
had allowed him really to get to the bottom of the Arian
affair. Slowly he began to see that even the limited objec-
tive he had set himself—not the eternal truth about the
Trinity, searched to its depths, but general peace on the

surface of things—still eluded him. Perhaps, too, the concentration of his own faith on God the Father to the neglect of Christ affected his judgment, or the widespread parallels drawn between the divine and the earthly realms—parallels favoring a monarchic, subordinationist theology. Constantine could hardly think of one of his own princes claiming an equal share in his power. Moreover, with Ossius gone, other influences came forward. Helena had honored Lucian, the teacher of Arius and others, with a church; Constantine's sister-in-law Basilina was actively pro-Arian; his sister Constantia supported Eusebius of Nicomedia. All three, then, were in the same camp.

So Arius was forgiven, and Eusebius of Nicomedia, too, in about 328; and henceforth to the end of the reign the two Eusebii together enjoyed a kind of primacy. Their hand can be surmised in a number of minor events, and occasionally can be more certainly detected—as against Eustathius.

Head of one of the greatest cities of the East, his removal was the grand prize. He struck back in speeches, letters to potential allies, and a pamphlet warfare; but Eusebius managed to show that these writings were themselves heretical, or nearly so, and on top of this, a woman, babe in arms, was induced or paid to confess that the bishop was its father. A large synod convened in Antioch to condemn and depose him (*ca.* 330). Reports reached Constantine of disorders in the streets. His resentment was aroused by Eustathius' intractability and alleged slights on the queen mother. The sentence of condemnation thus received his support, and two of his counts rode off to Antioch to oversee the election of a new bishop. Eusebius headed the list of candidates, and Eustathius campaigned to reclaim his office; but the former soon withdrew his name, the

latter got nowhere, and victory fell to a relative non-
entity—needless to say, an Arianist.

Athanasius continued in his public utterances and letters
to speak of Eustathius' party as the rightful church of
Antioch; he would not let Arius enter Egypt; and in the
flurry of arrests and riots that disturbed the province, he
made good use of popular enthusiasm and armed support
from the Alexandrian garrison. But his defiance gave the
Meletians within Egypt, and the Arianists without, the very
weapon they needed. His power and independence in Egypt
seemed to threaten the throne itself. Earlier accusations
that he had raised a tax on his own authority and aided a
suspected traitor now took on a certain credibility in the
emperor's mind; and, by coincidence, a pretender did arise
for a brief moment about this time in Cyprus, as a reminder of the instability that might yet tear the empire
apart.

Against this background, some especially dramatic event
was sought to complete Athanasius' downfall. First a man
was found willing to disappear for a while. Athanasius was
accused of murdering him and using his body for sorcery.
Things looked black indeed until the murderer found his
victim—alive! Though still, when he produced him perfectly
healthy in court, the Meletians "called Athanasius a wizard
and said he had used his magic arts to fool men's eyes."

Ever inventive, the Meletians also had on hand a woman
claiming to have been a vowed virgin. Athanasius had rav-
ished her, she said. As she could not recognize him in court,
her testimony did not carry much weight. But we may well
believe that orthodox churchmen in Egypt had intimidated,
beaten, arrested, or deposed from office their Meletian opponents; and Arianists were still barred from the province.
All these charges and the necessary witnesses and deposi-

tions were ready for a council called at Caesarea, and the target of them, by his pleas and delays, only persuaded Constantine to reschedule the council for Tyre (early 335). Constantine sent a count to preside, and to see fair play and decent order.

The Council of Tyre instead followed a more predictable pattern. Athanasius' enemies packed it with their votes and locked out his supporters. A fact-finding committee, dispatched to Egypt, consisted solely of Arianists. So Athanasius, after whatever struggles and protests he could manage, fled the assembly for Constantinople. While the council was condemning him *in absentia*, he was on his way to the emperor, whom he convinced momentarily of the illegality of what was going on at Tyre. Constantine ordered the council (now moved to Jerusalem) to come to him in his capital. Only a few, including the Eusebii, obeyed, but their report that Athanasius had threatened to cut off the grain supply to Constantinople seems to have been the last straw. He was promptly banished to Trèves where he remained till a new reign.

We might wish the story of Arianism shorter, certainly less confused, were it not for what it tells about the participants. So far as concerns the Church, the most obvious phenomenon was the degree to which its inwardness, that is, the intangible essence of Christianity, had been absorbed into the body of secular politics. We may instance Eusebius of Nicomedia, intriguing at court; Athanasius bending the local garrison to his own ends; or Arius setting to popular tunes, to be sung in the streets, the more understandable parts of his inflammatory doctrine. There is nothing surprising in this development. Once the Church could come out into the open, surely its behavior was bound to change. Constantine encouraged this. Synods approxi-

mated to imperial hearings on appeal, episcopal courts to
governors', sees (by a canon of Nicaea) to the boundaries
of existing municipalities, and ecclesiastical regalia and ceremonies to those of the palace. The identical process
influenced the effort of individuals or parties to impose
their own dogma on everyone else. They became, quite
naturally, politicians.

Some were destroyed by the change. Politics, as was
said before, became for them an end in itself. But not all.
Among the majority whose sincerity is obvious, we may
return again to the start of it all: Arius. Stripped of office,
homeless, fought over, and forced to bend an uncom-
promising intellect to party purposes and half-truths, he
endured even through a long illness. Constantine, almost in
the manner of Lactantius, writes to him a taunting description of himself (333):

Take heed, everyone take heed, how sad he sounds, when
pierced by the serpent's sting [*i.e.*, the Devil's], how his
veins and flesh, injected with the poison, shoot terrible pains,
how his whole wasted body flows away [in dysentery], how
he is filled with filth and dirt and wretchedness and pallor
and trembling and a thousand ills, how horrible a skeleton
he has grown, how disgustingly dirty and tangled his hair,
how half-dead all over, how feeble the look of his eyes,
bloodless his face, and how emaciated he is from his cares.

When, three years later, he was present at Constantinople
for hearings, he was seized with an attack of diarrhea,
excused himself from his companions, and died actually in
a latrine. Athanasius (and the emperor as well, he says) of
course regarded this as divine punishment for Arius' sins.
The last recorded fragments of this repellent, tragic person

are, "I am raised aloft on delight, I leap and bound with joy, I am on wings;" and, "I die."

For a while Constantine was reconciled to Arius, and then turned against him more savagely than ever. For a while he was set against Eusebius of Nicomedia, and called him "that shameless servant of the Devil," and other names, but that relationship changed, too. He blew hot and cold on Athanasius, now praising him in a letter which he commanded specifically to be published throughout Alexandria, now threatening a personal visit to the city to throw him off his episcopal throne. His official rescripts and decrees grow increasingly angry. His subjects will not come to his councils when he calls them, they will not cease from their perpetual disagreements, they try to hoodwink him with tricks of language and secret plots. His explosions of violent vilification mingle ridiculously with pleas of *homonoia*.

But the ultimate cause of his frustration here is what it was in his troubles with the Donatists. Commanding extraordinary resources for the control of police, labor, armies, currency, finances, promotions, public building—in sum, the external structure of life—in his role of emperor, and triumphantly fitted to this role by nature and achievements, he could not penetrate to deeper beliefs. Neither his office nor his mind gave him the power to lead within the fellowship to which he had been converted. He could claim at most to have been "appointed by God over those *outside* the Church."

A

B   *C*   *D*

PLATE IX The emperor in the news: Constantine's *liberalitas* to the people of Rome (A, from the Arch; see Plate V); his *Adventus*, led by Victoria, followed by Virtus (B, the reverse side of the coin in Plate III, B); C, his *Gloria* won in battle over barbarians; and his speech or *Adlocutio* to his troops (D, the reverse of the coin in Plate III, C).

PLATE X Helena with her jewel box, on a fresco of ca. 321 from Treves, and on a coin of 325, with her earrings and pearl necklace.

Plate XI Constantius II.

PLATE XII The royal family: Fausta as the Well-being of the State, with Constantine II and Constantius II (A-B); Crispus, Most Noble Caesar (C) and with Constantine II (D); the latter and Constantius II as Hope of the State, flanking their father (E). Note Constantine's nimbus or halo, and how suddenly the children grow up, all the coins dating to the 320's!

PLATE XIII San Giovanni, in a seventeenth century fresco.

PLATE XIV Saint Peter's before the seventeenth century restoration.

PLATE XV   Remains of the basilica in Rome.

PLATE XVI Reconstruction of the basilica in Rome.

X

THE SPIRIT OF CONSTANTINE'S GOVERNMENT

Anyone could have predicted that Constantine after 315 would lavish energy and money on church building in the East. His record at Trèves and at Rome pointed in that direction, and Constantinople's rising splendors proved that he had not yet satisfied the ambition that every emperor felt, to leave behind him visible monuments of his greatness. At first, reorganization of what he had conquered kept him busy; next, his capital, and doctrinal disputes, and the Nicene council; and then his celebration of his *vicennalia*, beginning with the bishops' banquet and ending with his trip to Rome. On the way back, danger (as he thought) opened like a crevasse at his feet. He detected his eldest son and his wife in treason. Crispus was suffocated in a baths building at Pola, a few days' journey from Aquileia; Fausta, not long afterwards, at Trèves (326). Nothing is known of their crime, unless one wants to believe the story of their adultery. Their names were chiseled away from stone inscriptions and a discreet or horrified silence settled on their memories.

According to pagan sources, hostile but not necessarily wrong, Helena's distress or sense of guilt over what had happened prompted a visit to the Holy Land in this year. Her movements cannot be traced in detail down to her death in 329 or 330, but she evidently spent some time in the area. Wherever she passed she distributed gifts—to some, silver, to some, clothes. She amnestied convicts and exiles and worshipped in the churches; she sought out the company of nuns to do them honor, and the poor, to relieve their distress. But she was, beyond this, the first pilgrim. She had been told in a dream to look for the site of the Holy Sepulcher, and succeeded in finding it, hidden under a mound of earth and a shrine of Aphrodite. With the discovery of the Sepulcher, the True Cross was found also; of which, a century later, it was related that its nails were sent to Constantine to be made into a bit for his war-horse, and its wood proved able to heal the sick. Constantine wrote to Macarius, bishop of Jerusalem, that he had cleared the site "by the command of God" and that Macarius was to oversee the construction of a fitting memorial. The vicar of the praetorian prefect and the governor of Palestine had been alerted to supply workmen, material, and funds for the project as Macarius might direct, "so that the basilica may be not only better than others anywhere else, but such that in all respects the beauties of every city shall yield to this building." "Hurry," Constantine urges; he sends architects; and he particularly wants to know if the ceiling will be suited to gilding. When completed, the enormous complex included a porticoed courtyard containing the rock of Calvary and the Sepulcher enclosed in a circular shrine, the Anastasis. The courtyard was attached to the rotunda, in turn joined to a four-aisled basilica fronted on the east by an atrium. The emperor enriched this structure with rare marbles, gold foil on the ceiling, objects of silver, and so on, in overwhelming abundance. He took great pride in the achievement, and when Eusebius of Nicomedia expressed some interest in seeing it, he and his retinue were provided with public transportation for the trip—during which they stopped off at Antioch to conspire against Eustathius. At its dedication, the basilica was filled with the envoys who had been attending the Council of Tyre, and who were instructed to swell the crowds and dignify the ceremonies at Jerusalem. They used their further sessions in the city to pursue their condemnation of Athanasius.

Helena through Constantine also put up a basilica (the Eleona) on the Mount of Olives, and (the Nativity) over the cave at Bethlehem where, variant traditions said, Christ had been born. A fourth basilica rose near the Mamre Oak in Hebron where God spoke to Abraham and where, at the request of the emperor's mother-in-law, a count was ordered to clean away all the pagan altars and cults that had grown up, and to supervise the construction of a church. The emperor's intent at the four sites was to bring into prominence the places celebrated in the history of Christianity, and to this end the churches in the Holy Land, like those of St. Peter and St. Paul in Rome, combined accommodations for regular worship and for commemoration. Constantine never saw the Holy Land, but through his and Helena's and Eutropia's work it became, within a generation or two, the center for Christian pilgrimage that it has ever since remained.

In his own efforts to provide Christian worship with a suitable architectural setting, he circularized the eastern bishops in 324, instructing them to repair what had been ruined or neglected under "that serpent" Licinius. The praetorian prefect and governors stood ready to provide everything necessary in the way of a work force and money. One of his counts, Joseph of Tiberias in Palestine, having been interestingly converted from Judaism by "divine visions of every kind," obtained drafts on the treasury and special authority to go about in predominantly Jewish regions erecting churches. He started with an abandoned temple which the locals were in course of converting into a bathhouse; but they hexed his efforts at preliminary lime-burning "by certain enchantments and juggleries." Joseph got the fires in the kilns to catch by dousing them with water over which he had made the sign of the cross, at which the crowd exclaimed, "One is the God who helps the Christians!" So he finished the job.

In Antioch, next to the palace, Constantine built the Golden Octagon, a church with a gilded roof, extraordinary height, and the optimistically given name of "Harmony"; another rose in Nicomedia, another in Drepanum, where Constantine occasionally enjoyed the hot springs and where his mother had been born. It was rechristened Helenopolis in her honor (327), as Arles and Cirta became Constantina, and Maiuma, Constantia, after the emperor's sister, and because of the town's conversion to Christianity.

In Tiberias, Maiuma, and Mamre we touch on a more aggressive side of imperial policy. It aimed at physically supplanting paganism. His soldiers razed famous temples and sanctuaries in various cities—of Cilicia, Phoenicia, Egypt, and Syria—because of particularly offensive beliefs centered in them, and on their ruins churches rose; temple doors and roofs of bronze were ripped away to be melted into coins; so, likewise, gold and silver statues or ornaments on cult images. It must be said, however, that Constantine was as ready to confiscate the houses of Christian worship, if they were heretical, Donatist, Valentinian, Cataphrygian, or other; and the instances of actual destruction of pagan sanctuaries or idols are very few, scattered, and almost all dated to the last half-dozen years of the reign. Any more radical action would be surprising from a man who

had witnessed, from both sides of the fence, the failure of
the persecutions, and who in his official capacity maintained
many ties with his past. Some have been mentioned. He
went on appointing pagans to his government, even to his
personal entourage. To his very last breath he remained
head of the established state cults, *pontifex maximus*. It was
symbolic of a compromise—an inoffensive concession to
ancient custom, yet intimately connected with the office of
emperor. The latter aspect perhaps explains the retention
of the title. For the same reason, since it so closely con-
cerned his role, he tolerated a certain degree of emperor
worship. He replied to a petition of his subjects in Umbria,
in the latter half of his reign, that they might indeed establish, independently of certain former associates, religious
celebrations in honor of the Flavian family. Games and
gladiatorial combats would be permitted if not "polluted
with superstition." Constantine must have had in mind what
he abhorred in some of the temples he had razed: filthy
rituals—morally filthy, like temple prostitution, or tangi-
bly, for example, the inspection of entrails or the bloodbath
of the *taurobolium*. Third- and fourth-century Christian
writers execrate both; but veneration of his clan involved
neither—hence its encouragement in Africa (above, p. 102),
and the priests of the cult sometimes encountered quite
openly and proudly on inscriptions. It was more a matter
of patriotism than of worship; and the emperor paid for
the chapel.

A sort of no-man's-land divided religious from secular
affairs. Conservative where he could be, Constantine, in
this area, made as few changes as possible. Neither he nor
the Church, as we know from its canons, forbade the holding of municipal priesthoods, because they were more like
magistracies. On the other hand, certain purely secular acts

were filled with religious implications. Thus it was that
Constantine could paradoxically encourage men to hold
the post of *flamen* (in 337) while forbidding crucifixion.

Other aspects of his legislation at first sight seem puzzling, too. As a Christian, surely he might be expected to
speak like one. The fact is, he did, but in the language and
with the ideas that belonged to his time; and he was not a
saint. When thwarted, his rage burst forth in shouts and
imprecations. "Let the greedy hands of the civil secretaries
forbear, let them forbear, I say," begins a law of 331 directed at administrative venality. And it goes on, "If after
due warning they do not cease, they shall be cut off by the
sword." He means it literally. Or again, for parents acces-
sory to the seduction of their daughter, "the penalty shall
be that the mouth and throat of those who offered induce-
ment to evil shall be closed by pouring in molten lead."
Horrible; but no more so than the descriptions that Lactantius supplies in his account *Of the Deaths of the Persecutors*,
dwelling with a kind of joyful fascination on the disgusting
torments in which Galerius or some other emperor died. It
was a brutal age, and men attributed brutality to God. His
punishments justified equal horrors on earth, in a good
cause. Witness the (to us) perfectly repellent pleasure that
Constantine took in the sufferings of Arius. They were the
instrument of instruction, as he saw it. Witness the contradiction only apparent in a law of 315 or 316, declaring it
quite proper to condemn a man to death in the arena but
not to brand him on the face, "which is shaped in the
likeness of heavenly beauty"! The emperor's ideas of
Christianity make sense only when they are considered in a
much wider context than the religious; for obviously whatever he learned from Ossius or Eusebius or Lactantius did

not displace but only joined a thousand other influences forming, in their totality, late Roman culture.

Constantine invoked the death penalty quite freely, but so had his predecessors and so did his sons after him. He made it a capital crime to distrain for debt on a man's slaves or draught animals, to collect taxes beyond the authorized amount, or for a free woman to have sexual intercourse with a slave. That last followed long precedent, aimed not so much at preserving the morals as the ranks of society. Throughout his reign, Constantine's decrees blended with others earlier and later to mark off and deal separately with senators, equestrians, the free and great (*honestiores*), the free but humble (*humiliores*), and mere slaves at the bottom of the heap. He upheld the privileges of each, he enforced the obligations of each. New subdivisions appeared, honorific among *patricii* or burdensome among farmers (*coloni*) bound to the plot of land where they were born. In much of this, his innate conservatism can be seen, for social distinctions had long been rooted in Roman life and law. Sons were not to revolt against their fathers nor freedmen to give offense to their former masters. Old Cato the Censor would have recognized and applauded such rules. Minors were to remain in their dependent status, partly for their own protection, and women, too, whom Romans had never permitted to appear in a court. By an easy extension, under pressure of economic and administrative necessity, certain groups received legal definition—municipal senators or linen weavers—the better to discharge their duties. Some of these function groups have been mentioned above: shipowners, builders, even Christian priests, whose exemptions and state-supplied dole came to them in recognition of the part they played in

securing general peace and prosperity. "For," Constantine
reminds his proconsul in 313, "when these persons offer
the Divinity's supreme cult, they seem also to contribute
immensely to the commonwealth." His way of looking at
things his subjects could perfectly understand. It underlies,
while robbing of any significant Christianness, all those
measures already surveyed at various points, where he legislated in favor of the Church, and where the spiritual
consequences of his conversion are often sought.

Toward two groups he turned a kinder face Was this
for Christianity's sake? The first were slaves. When crown
land was broken up for sale, they were not to be separated,
husband from wife, parent from child. It is very likely
though not demonstrable that he here speaks under the
influence of religion. At the same time, however, he, like
individual churches and churchmen, owned slaves and defended the institution. If he limited masters' rights of cruel
punishment, he found no crime in the death of a slave in
consequence of a beating, administered for due cause. As
for the second group, *humiliores*, that is, simply men who
held no special office, he repeatedly defends them against
oppression; but, like his successors for centuries, what he
intends is not so much the strengthening of the poor for
their own sake as the weakening of *potentiores*, men such
as the Bassi and Anicii whose wealth and influence was
rising like a wall between the emperor and the mass of his
own subjects.

In several aspects, then—harshness of penalties, regard
for the past, defense of subordination of one type of person to another, and the tendency to see people as members
of some group performing a certain job for society—the
character of Constantine's legislation grows out of the

times. He rarely approaches a problem as a Christian, rather as a whole man of the fourth century, of whatever religion.

But innovation can be detected giving his legislation its own special quality. This entailed a departure from Roman legal traditions. The subject is not easy to explain. While the Greeks poured their intellectual energy into philosophy, the Romans turned their equal powers to the law; and since everyone is sure that he is a pretty fair philosopher, though entertaining doubts about his competence as a lawyer, the Roman achievement is little understood. By the third century it had transformed a people's social and political wisdom into a discipline distinct, refined, and subtle—not so much in the dealings of the state with private citizens as in their dealings with each other. Naturally, cruder procedures—the body of "vulgar" or customary law—governed decisions of small courts in small towns, wherever Romanization had not penetrated deeply. The eastern provinces in particular had their own legal traditions, generally Greek. Under Constantine the doors were opened partway to the intrusion of this alien body.

Consider the rules laid down in 320 for the better treatment of prisoners. It is a long text concerning details of incarceration. Sufficient to quote only one sentence representative of the whole.

Nor surely will the prisoner be made to endure the darkness of the inner parts, but to revive in the enjoyment of the light, and when night doubles the guard he shall be taken to the forecourts of the jail and into healthy quarters, and on the return of day again, at the sun's first rising, shall be led promptly to the open light, lest he perish from the pains of jail that are considered wretched for the innocent though for the guilty not severe enough.

What strikes the reader are the rather long-winded, explanatory, adjectival expressions employed here, characteristic of Constantine in his letters, speeches, and public proclamations, and standing midway along the road to a fully inflated Byzantinism. Did the same style belong in what was intended as no more than a set of instructions to semiliterate jailers? In avoiding a flat, dry style, or the repetition of the same word, accuracy yielded to false elegance, and intelligibility to periphrasis. As he distrusted philosophers and theologians, so Constantine also distrusted legal technicians, and introduced into his government the rich prose taught by rhetoricians such as Nazarius and Lactantius.

The effect was baneful. Legists were hard enough to find anyway, in this undereducated period. To bestow imperial favor on loose wording, inexact synonyms, and contored sentence structure undermined the influence of really competent experts, and opened the way to all sorts of arbitrary interpretation. On the good side, this sometimes meant equity as against a bureaucrat's strictness—*aequitas, humanitas, iustitia* (as opposed to *ius*), even the more explicit *lenitas, indulgentia, clementia,* and similar words sprinkled through the emperor's laws, permitting an occasional ray of Christian mercy to shine through. On the bad side, while there was no conscious intent of challenging tradition, in fact the professionalism of the past came under the attack of fuzzier concepts that prevailed in everyday, non-technical relationships, and especially in customary law. Since the center of government had shifted permanently eastward by the 320's, it was Hellenistic custom that showed most clearly in Constantinian legislation. Its influence, once established, continued to grow under his successors.

The East was also the home of divine kingship, perpetuated through Hellenistic monarchies. The Romans found in it a treasury of ideas and symbols. Constantine was the first to adopt the jeweled diadem (326), in its final form a double strand of pearls around his head; and he was the first emperor, too, to adopt that upward tilt of the face and raised eyes that had developed in the iconography of Alexander the Great. Eusebius mentions a painting in this style hung over the palace gates, and detects in it the posture of a Christian in prayer; but the evidence that survives is mostly to be found rather in coins, of 325 and later, which reveal a good knowledge, sometimes exact imitation, of models issued by Greek kings five or six centuries earlier. They were portrayed as if gazing at some higher source of power and inspiration. Incidentally, the influence of these coins combined with other currents of change to produce a softening of imperial portraiture, a less harsh, less linear idealization of the ruler. The soldier-savior of Tetrarchic times could melt into a more beneficent image, though no less filled with the divine. The outline of Constantine's great broken beak of a nose and prognathous jaw softened—the chin perhaps in part because he was growing stout in his later years. He took to wearing his hair longer, too. His nephew Julian makes fun of his fondness for rich foods and his dependence on the comb and curling tongs. But hair reaching to the shoulders belonged equally to the image of Alexander and of superhuman force.

Besides their official titles as Most Perfect, Outstanding, Most Eminent, and the rest, strictly regulated according to rank, Constantine's servants were addressed by him with various other terms of high courtesy, ordinarily as Your Gravity, but also as Your Authority, Your Devotion, etc.

Himself he referred to as Our Clemency (the favorite word), or Our Wisdom, or less often as Our Piety, Prudence, Majesty, etc. All parts of his office, of course, from his audience hall to the hem of his robe, were sacred; all acts praised as divine. A din of adulation filled the palace. But within it, contradictorily, reigned silence, enforced by the newly created crops of ushers named *silentiarii*. The paradox is exactly mirrored in a number of laws, some of them complaining about the excessive quantity of minor business referred right up to the emperor, some of them on the other hand complaining more angrily about the matters that are being kept from him. Officials must not edit petitions to suppress hints of misdoing, subjects are to have free access to the throne. The elaborate remoteness of the emperor that guards him from plots and bestows on him some of the mystery and holiness of a god in a temple also prevents him from finding out what is going on in the world he rules. Against this isolation he very emphatically protests:

To all provincials: If anyone anywhere in any rank or office believes he can truly and clearly establish anything, against any of my governors, counts, retinue, or court, that seems not to have been properly and justly handled, let him come forward with courage and in safety, let him address himself to me. I myself will hear everything, I myself will judge, and if the matter is substantiated, I will avenge myself. Let him speak! If the matter is proven, as I said, I will avenge myself.

The scheme of government devised by Diocletian rested on the magistrates of many thousand towns and cities; over them, governors of more than a hundred provinces; next higher in authority, vicars of the praetorian prefects in charge of fourteen dioceses; next, praetorian prefects. Cutting through the various levels of the pyramid were special financial agencies. Constantine did little to change the lower or middle levels, but, as has been mentioned, he took away from the too powerful prefects the general control of personnel, vested henceforward in the Master of Offices; and he further reduced the sphere of praetorian prefects by giving to a Quaestor of the Sacred Palace the responsibility for records, charters, imperial directives, and the drafting of laws. With this office, the structure of administration in all major respects was complete, to last for centuries.

But hardly less important increases in the numbers of bureaucrats were accomplished in his reign, and two further innovations which affected the court. Counts (*comites*, literally "companions") appear first under Constantine as bearers of a formal rank and as members of the consistory (*consistorium*, meaning that everybody in it stood about while the emperor sat). "Consistory" itself is a new word for the supreme council, destined likewise for a long, long life. It brought together the heads of bureaus, the praetorian prefects, Master of Offices, and other ministers of state, including the two new treasury officers, Count of the Crown Properties, and Count of the Sacred Largesses. Also present would be the other innovation in the court, the Chief Chamberlain, a eunuch set over the *silentiarii* and the lesser staff of the emperor's, and of the quite separate empress', apartments. The Chief Chamberlain was so constantly in contact with the emperor and had such good opportunities of influencing him or of admitting or not admitting people to his presence that his position rapidly grew in importance. And because he was a eunuch, in an empire where deliberate castration was illegal, he and most of his underlings (not the *silentiarii*) originated in Armenia, Persia, or Scythia. They somehow got along with those other exotic figures in the imperial guard, the German barbarians. It is curious to think of the many languages whispered in the corridors by these palace troops and servants, while greater men unrolled their periods in Greek and Latin.

A final word should be said about Constantine's economic policy. It was traditional in his role and the most obvious of his responsibilities to see that his subjects had enough to eat. Rome's needs were well taken care of, Constantinople's newly supplied, and a dole was established for the citizens of Puteoli. That last deserved special favor owing to its part in funneling provisions from Egypt and Africa into central Italy. A famine in Syria in 334 produced riots and pillaging around Antioch. The state offered relief to be distributed through churches to the hungry. Eusebius refers quite unspecifically to the emperor's generous almsgiving and succor of widows, orphans, and beggars. In the West he several times remitted taxes to individual cities or provinces, both during and after his years spent in that part of the empire, and in 325 and 327 granted certain tax remissions to East and West alike. This was the period in which a vast amount of building was in process of completion in Rome and just under way in Constantinople and the Holy Land.

We have no means of determining where all the money came from, either in this time of particular extravagance or throughout a reign that was to be remembered as very free-spending. In the wake of the great war of 324, for which Licinius, like Maxentius and Carausius in similar straits, had had to tighten the screws of taxation, the eastern provinces can have brought little wealth to their conqueror—at least not for a few years. A generation later, perhaps as puzzled as we are, pagans tried to explain Constantine's well-stocked treasury by pointing to his pillage of temples. They may be right in mentioning, but not in emphasizing, this as a source of irregular income; it certainly cannot account for any large percentage of the emperor's wealth.

A better answer lies in brand new taxes (above, p. 86), in the severer and more rational system of collection established by Diocletian, and in the exaction of unremunerated services to the state. The device was as old as organized society, employed in the later Empire in a hundred areas of need. To describe it in any detail would draw us away from our subject proper into a general history of the third and fourth centuries; but repair of Constantinople's aqueducts, shipment of grain to both capitals, supply of manufactures to army and court, or the milling of flour and baking of bread, all being partially or wholly unpaid for, may be drawn from previous pages as illustrations of how the device worked. Another kind of illustration may be remembered, too. Those function groups mentioned earlier formed the operative parts of the system. Not only did the state dump many of its burdens on the shoulders of its citizens, but those who objected were dragged back in chains, to the post assigned them, by still other fellow citizens serving as unsalaried "volunteer" police. This last was one of the *munera* from which clergy were wisely exempted. Other duties in the list included the billeting of troops, road building, and local tax collection. It was a neat, sometimes cruelly neat, aspect of the whole mechanism of late Roman government that exemption itself became a sort of payment used by the emperor to "buy" new services.

Constantine did make a positive contribution to the economy which probably goes some way toward explaining the relative prosperity of his reign. He laid the foundations of a sound currency. Three metals circulated, as they had for centuries, each of them in various denominations: gold, silver, and bronze. In healthy times their interrelationships remained stable, and each could be exchanged with others according to the needs of large or small transactions. This was essential. The difference between an empire of market towns and an empire of cities, dependent on commerce, lay precisely in the existence of a coinage in which people had confidence. But confidence was severely shaken in the third century with the progressive debasement of one of its elements, silver, as the actual proportion of that metal in nominally pure coins sank abruptly to one or two per cent. The interrelationships among the metals being once destroyed, people took to barter—a pig for a pair of shoes, a half-pound of bronze for a jar of wine, coins being measured out by weight. In terms of a discredited currency, prices shot up, savings vanished, trade shrank into smaller circles. Though the economy did not collapse, indeed stood up surprisingly well, yet the losses and inconveniences proved deeply damaging to the state and private citizen alike.

In the generation before Constantine, and by Licinius as well, heroic efforts were made to restore sanity. New denominations appeared bearing new numbers on them to indicate in what ratio they were to stand with the old, and new valuations were announced even if they could not be enforced. Inflation swept them all away. The firmest element, gold, gradually emerged as the only practical basis for permanent recovery, and Diocletian turned to it with partial success. What Constantine did, in about 312, was to diminish the present gold coin to ¹⁄₇₂ of a pound, issuing it, moreover, with notable abundance, fineness, and consistent weight. This was the *solidus;* its sub-multiples were carats (24 *siliquae,* as they were called). When it had made its way and reputation in the market, repair of silver (*ca.* 323) could be attempted, though with limited results. Bronze never could be controlled, and prices expressed in it reached dizzying figures of 300,000 or 1,500,000.

Of most aspects of these monetary problems no clear picture can be recovered. It is certain, however, that the *solidus* stemmed the movement toward barter, ultimately terminated inflation, and made possible the gradual rebuilding of a money economy. It endured unaltered for many centuries, circulating throughout the Mediterranean, taking at last the name 'bezant' from its central place of issue, Byzantium or Constantinople.

In reviewing the record of Constantine's government, one notes how it develops on the foundation laid down by Diocletian. It is in many ways a work of completion—forceful, intelligent, thorough. One notes its predominant conservatism. But it is innovation that one naturally is most interested in finding; and surely Constantine differed from his predecessors principally in his conversion. In that, then, must lie the source of whatever is new. Yet the moral teachings of Christ had wrought no radical revolution. There is no evidence that more slaves were freed within the Christian community of the early fourth century than among pagans; that a feeling of brotherhood joined Arius to the beggars in the streets; or that Eusebius was readier to relieve poverty in Antioch than Pliny had been in his town of Comum, two hundred years before. Christianity, in short, in the influence it exerted on men's lives, in part responded and in part contributed to a complex

of ideas unfolding slowly even after the advent of a be-
liever to the throne; and Constantine therefore cannot be
looked to for the remaking of his world beyond all his
contemporaries.

What one does find is a person of a particular character
inheriting a governmental system with particular tenden-
cies of its own. He is by nature imperious, and the system
responds to that quality; he is short-tempered when balked
or disobeyed, and it provides precedents and instruments
for severity. The confidence that he is right readily takes
form in the magnification of his office, in the unfolding of a
richer ceremonial, in the pomposity of bureaucratic language; and when he aspires to glorify God, he may well do
so—history tells him—by building churches. The individual's intent and nature may say what they will, but
they must speak only through the mask of the role.

XI

THE COURT

In the mind's eye the ancient world is a pale one:
temples, togas, statues. That picture is quite wrong. White-
washed the poor man's house in the Mediterranean, to
throw off the heat, and gray his clothes of undyed wool
and cotton; but whoever could afford it, at least in the
later Empire, aimed at a very different style. If the setting
of life is to be reconstructed, it must be in good high
rooms (none of those little low-ceilinged boxes that most
of us must live in) lined with cheerful frescoes—panels
of green framed in yellow or of red on blue, with loops
and garlands of flowers running wild across them; in a
central courtyard, the same variety of red or green or yellow marble glistening under the water of a pool or foun-
tain; even the walls that faced the street painted, or
decorated with balconies and window boxes. So too with
the inhabitants: the richer, the brighter. Some borrowed
from retainers and professional performers the fashion of
whole dyed garments; but that was less common than
embroidered strips, squares, and circles sewn to the shoulders or sleeves, down the front closing of a cloak, or along
its hem. The strips had merely ornamental designs on them,
whereas the larger patches, up to a foot across, might show
a hunt scene, gods or goddesses, perhaps a little portrait of
some historical figure, perhaps a member of the royal family. And jewelry enjoyed great popularity (plate X). On

this, as also on objects for the table, the goldsmith lavished a skill amply patronized. His art is one of the few that suffered no falling off, but rather rose to new heights, amidst the general decline of Rome.

The fact is characteristic. Late Roman invention, though limited or altogether lacking in many areas, had new refinements of ceremonial to offer in the homes of the well-to-do as, more grandly, in the palace. It elaborated the formality of parades, of *adventus*, of horse racing, of trials, in short, of any public occasion. It elaborated the show-off parts of domestic dwellings, producing here and there throughout the empire reception halls in mansions of incredible size. They have been discovered in Syria, North Africa, southwestern France, and Sicily, to name some specially well-known sites. And, like jewelry, third- and fourth-century architecture, within a certain range of objectives, flourished as never before. Especially it could overwhelm, through the height of vaults or through the unrelieved expanse of vast stretches of space. It stunned the eye with relentlessly repetitive, identical columns, coffers, or arches (plates VI, XIII, XIV). Illustrations have been given, in pages that dealt with the transformation of Trèves, Rome, Constantinople, and Jerusalem. What characterizes the building program in these cities, as likewise jewelry, costume, and ceremonial behavior, is the quality of display, the more exaggerated as developing against an increasingly bleak background.

In the foreground enter the actors: Constantine first, bearing the heavy role like the heavy robes of his supreme power with dignity, even with a somewhat complacent serenity. As he approaches his tricennalia—the celebration of his thirtieth year of rule which begins and ends (July 335, 336) in brilliant fireworks of congratulatory eloquence—he is in his fifties. His figure is heavyset (plate IIG), his complexion flushed. He wears his curly hair long. Around him cluster the men and women whom he sees every day and who most directly affect his life.

They form an outer ring of palace servants from the northeastern corners of the realm, of guards from the northwestern—Armenian eunuchs, Frankish troopers. Closer in are the great persons of his government, a few lingering for years in his immediate entourage, most of them coming and going to and from appointments in the provinces. All but a few are known to us as names only. Some of them establish a line later famous, like the father of St. Ambrose, or the grandfather of Theodosius. Some spring from already noble families like the *potentiores* of Rome, some have risen entirely on their own merits. Count Joseph was such a one; another was Ablabius, of humble lineage, a Cretan by birth, converted to Christianity, and all-powerful in the court. He acquired wide estates in Bithynia, passed through the vicariate of Italy (315) to the praetorian prefecture (329-337); held the consulship with one of the Bassi in 331; saw his daughter betrothed to Prince Constans and actually married later to the king of Persia. The emperor, before his death, appointed him adviser and guardian to the young Constantius, who was promptly rid of him. For his long tenure of influence there are several parallels in Constantine's reign, during which the stability of government seems to have been one of the things wisely aimed at.

Hermogenes was also from an eastern province, a deep student of philosophy who had entered government as legal expert and whom Constantine inherited upon his victory in 324. He became apparently Constantine's Quaestor of the Sacred Palace, going on to service under Constantius, and dying as praetorian prefect of the East in 361. Like him in learning was Strategius, elegantly bilingual. Constantine drew instruction in Christian doctrine from him, but chiefly admired his cultivation, nicknaming him Musonianus. He became count and held many offices in this reign and the next, down to the 350's or 360's. Thirdly, we may mention Annius Tiberianus, a Christian but schooled in Plato, called by St. Jerome "a learned man." He served as count in several capacities, as vicar of Spain, and (predecessor to St. Ambrose's father) as praetorian prefect of Gaul (336). Though his book on Socrates is lost, four of his shorter poems survive, one beginning prettily,

Through the fields there went a river; down the
  airy glen it wound,
Smiling mid its radiant pebbles, decked with flowering
  plants around.
*Dark-hued laurels waved above it close by myrtle greeneries**

In a second he preaches against the evils of gold, "at whose enticement the unholy sword often flashes, drawn from the scabbard." "All guilt is hidden under gold, by gold all righteousness is betrayed." The reminder in an era of outrageously venal government no doubt pleased an emperor who, in his own calmer moments, had instructed his officials that "you can't take it with you," while at other moments he threatened to chop off the hands of any who accepted a bribe. For all these fulminations, dishonesty went on growing more and more blatant and entrenched.

Optatianus Porphyrius, dubiously Christian, has appeared above. He became urban prefect in Rome (329;

---

*Trans. by. J. W. Duff, *Minor Latin Poets* (1934), p. 559.

again in 333). Much of his work has come down to us, including the inglorious lines that he addressed from exile to "the tireless condescension of Your Clemency." He tickled his imperial audience with poems where certain letters had been picked out in red in a regular pattern to spell, like a crossword puzzle, the chi-rho, or "Omnipotent progenitor," or "Division joined," or "Son and Father and Holy Spirit, One, Hear my prayer," eliciting from Constantine the reassurance that, even if "Latin eloquence is stilled since the rustic Mantuan" (Vergil, of course), and even if "to the genius of some, the patronage of emperors was lacking which is wont to irrigate and nourish minds devoted to erudition, very much as a stream drawn down from the brow of a cliffy path softens the parched furrows with gushing rills, yet in my epoch an indulgent hearing attends those who speak and write, just like a gentle breeze. In sum, I will not fail to give deserved acknowledgment to such pursuits" as "this new kind of verse," whose secrets lie hidden in different-colored letters. Tricks pleased him. He liked the line written of himself, *quem divus genuit Constantius induperator.* The syllables of the five words increase in number, 1, 2, 3, 4, 5. Such devices as Optatianus Porphyrius practised and carried through whole poems had originated in Alexandria long ago, entered Latin only in this late period, and, needless to say, appealed to the shallowest taste—perhaps it would be truer to say, the tastes of men with little time for reading of any sort.

Two points emerge from this short roster of Constantine's closer associates: He valued Christianity and cultivation. Both points deserve discussion, with the addition of a few more names in its course.

As we have seen, Eusebius enjoyed imperial favor and received certain confidences which he duly reported after

337 in his essay *On the Life of Constantine.* There is record of other, relatively intimate contacts—a pungent rebuke to a rigorist, veneration shown to a scarred confessor, or unusual condescension to Church leaders individually in the court or summoned there in numbers for some special purpose. All of the figures we know anything about, incidentally, were years older than the emperor—Acesius, Paphnutius, Ossius, Eusebius, Lactantius, Alexander—because they lived in a society that respected age and bestowed honor in the Church (as very clearly in government) strictly according to seniority. Younger men had to wait for prominence.

The advent of a Christian to the throne vastly expanded the wealth, responsibilities, and consequently the rapidity of advancement in the Church. The generations after Constantine felt the benefit. But secular careers opened up to Christians as well. Constantine displayed a definite bias in their direction. If it was not so thoroughgoing as Eusebius says, at any rate we cannot easily find someone in a high position who was demonstrably non-Christian, except in Rome. The old capital had its own rules which might be broken after the 320's, but not entirely abolished. Its leading families did not willingly accept religious innovation, nor could they be denied a chance at positions of power that reached beyond Italy to other provinces. They thus constituted an important area of non-conformity within an administration to which their emperor would have preferred to give a completely Christian character. A second such was the army—doubtless also all sorts of resistant enclaves in the state where, little known to us, for one reason or another, change could not be hurried.

In the very heart of favor, however, quite notable pagans appear, rising above the emperor's usual prejudice against

them. Sopater, Greek rhetorician and Neoplatonist, moved
to Constantinople after the death of his master Iamblichus.
He attracted Constantine's attention and enjoyed a privileged position in the palace for some years. Another courtier grew envious. Ablabius accused him of having "chained
the winds" that should have brought the grain fleet, and
of thus having caused a shortage in the city. It was the
kind of charge easily credited in days when wise men did
indeed push their curiosity past philosophy into magic. For
this, or for some reason that our pagan source suppresses,
Constantine put Sopater to death. A second Neoplatonist
and rhetorician, Nicagoras, fared better. Like Sopater, he
came to notice a year or two after Constantine's conquest of the East. Like his own grandfather before him,
he held the official chair of sophistics at Athens. The family's fame in learning and letters reached back farther still.
He was really too distinguished to ignore. So it was with
Constantine's gracious permission and help that he led a
company of scholars on a voyage of research into Egypt
in 326—pagan research into the oracles and shrines, it
should be emphasized, and Nicagoras himself a torch-
bearer of the Eleusinian Mysteries. At Athens as at Rome,
history was to show over the next century or so how
deeply intertwined were the various parts of classical
culture, its priests with its philosophers. Sopater and Nicagoras illustrate this wider phenomenon. Only their great
reputation for wisdom and eloquence overcame the emper-
or's aversion to their religion.

Which brings us to our second point, the level of cultivation under Constantine. The Tetrarchs came from a
backward region of the empire. Rough men, they and
their appointees had no use for fancy education. That deficiency historians could not forgive. But even among those

writers who did not share Constantine's Christianity he
earned approval for the quite different spirit of his reign.
The nucleus of a state university at Constantinople demonstrated his enlightenment; so did annual state shipments
of grain for the historical center of higher studies, Athens,
and support of the school of rhetoric at Autun. Legislation
of about 324 on behalf of professors of grammar, rhetoric,
and medicine in whatever town they taught granted to
their persons and property exemption from *munera*, and
placed them on a par with clergy in this respect. Surely no
higher privilege could have been asked for them.

Such an act of grace had something paradoxical about
it, for as everyone knew, classical culture was first cousin
to paganism. The Church had already confronted that
supremely complicated relationship, and tested its dangers;
yet here was Constantine seeming to ignore it. It was
strange that so convinced a convert as he should extend
to men like Nicagoras and Sopater a patronage usually reserved for Christian circles. Stranger still, in our eyes, that
the prefecture of Rome and similar great offices should
have been held by dedicated amateurs, some, professionally
trained masters, of literature. The times, however, smiled
on the cult of letters. To speak and write with elegance
according to rules long refined earned incredible rewards,
not merely in the form of a bluestockinged audience or a
patron, but through the applause of masses of supporters
in public lecture halls, through opportunities to become a
millionaire, or through rapid advancement for this talent
alone to the topmost levels of government. The less common the talent in this age, the more prized, even in administrative posts where different skills made better sense.
Religious loyalty itself had to yield to its claims, had Constantine been personally immune to its attractions.

Quite to the contrary, he put himself to school, rather late in life, in the art of the rhetoricians. Eusebius gave him high marks for effort. Other writers, among them pagans, joined the chorus of somewhat cautious praise, though one is unkind enough to describe him as "zealous for eloquence which, as his slow wits prevented him from attaining it, he grudged to others." Both this and Eusebius' assessment are correct. Constantine obviously did aspire to fine style, and did fail to reach it. One illustration may be drawn from a long letter of 330 on the subject of episcopal elections, opening with a confused apostrophe to *homonoia*, continuing with the disarming remark, "Perhaps it may appear a mystery to you, what on earth this prologue to my address means," and concluding with the hope that the parties may be reconciled.

From the collision of the disputants sparks and flames result. As I would please both God and yourselves and as I would live to enjoy your prayers, I love you and the haven of your gentleness. Since you expelled that source of corruption, you have brought in *homonoia* in its place by your usual goodness, planting a secure trophy, running a celestial course towards the light, and, so to speak, with an iron rudder. For this cause, take on board the uncorruptible cargo; for all that defiled the ship is bailed out like bilgewater.

With the law on prison conditions quoted in the preceding chapter, this piece of prose shows how the emperor's hand grew stiff and clumsy in the composition of sentences meant to achieve the proper level of brilliance. Just as in architecture, contemporary costume, and courtly manners, the quality aimed at was display. Not everyone could combine that with good sense and good taste. Thus poor Constantine, at his self-conscious worst, mixes iron rudders, flames, trophies, horse races, and bilge water in a perfect chaos of metaphors, the absurdity of which quite hides the point he is trying to make. In contrast, when he speaks out naturally, he leaves no doubt about his meaning, whether it requires emphatic repetition—"Let them forbear, I say," or "Let him speak. If the matter is proven, as I said, I will avenge myself"—or whether it requires some vivid phrase—"the tongue of malice," "the greedy hands." Constantine is no fool, only the artificial bombast cultivated in his day sometimes made him seem so. His biographers must judge him in his own context, finding him guilty of nothing more than a maladroit straining for high fashion.

He made sure that his children would do better than he. Crispus' schooling must have been good, and Lactantius took over in the final stages. Little Constantine II could sign his name at the age of five, or thereabouts, to the joy of the court, and the royal nephews Delmatius and Hannibalianus studied under a famous Gallic rhetor, Exuperius, who later received as his reward a governorship in Spain. Another nephew, Julian, and Julian's friend Libanius, both hostile sources, nevertheless agree that Constantine took great pains to educate his sons in Latin letters, political science, and practical government.

Save in the matter of education, and Crispus' execution, the picture of Constantine as a father is totally blank. As a son, all that can be said is that he accorded to his mother prominence and independence. He had never betrayed his wife up to the moment when he became convinced that she had betrayed him. His worst detractors have no criticism to make of his private life. He appears to have been brought up strictly and to have imposed the same standards on his own circle, interpreted generously; for, as we have seen, he never hesitated to tell people of any rank, bishops included, what they should think on ethical questions.

His views originated not in his conversion, which came to him after his character had been formed, but in his upbringing and natural bent. If more general influences must be sought, perhaps they may be found in the peculiar code of the late Roman aristocracy that tolerated arrogance, cruelty, corruption, and insensitivity to the sufferings of the humble, while severely punishing all the vices, especially the sexual, harmful to the family. Contrast with Caesar's or Nero's day is striking. In the fourth century, whatever men's behavior in a public capacity, they jealously guarded the peace and purity of their homes.

Conversion nevertheless did have one effect. Constantine was determined that his own kin should be Christians, so Christians they became, Helena first (just when is not known) and his children as they grew up. His half brother Julius Constantius married for his second wife a Christian, Basilina, and his first wife was perhaps of the same faith, like their daughter who married Constantius II. Further relations and beliefs cannot be explored very far, for too little is known, but the indications are that the royal house had been quite cleansed of paganism within a decade or so of Constantine's own change of heart.

Constantine consolidated dynasticism. Disrupted by short reigns over much of the third century and necessarily repudiated by Diocletian, who had no son, this principle or political habit began to reassert its hold on men's loyalties in the period of transition from the Tetrarchy to the full founding of the Flavian fortunes, whether that be dated to the first Caesarship of Crispus in 317 or to the defeat of Licinius in 324. In preparation for that final test of strength, the Flavian princes had been pushed forward closer to the center of the stage to support their father's appeal (plate XII). Constantine II, only eight years old but seven years a Caesar, already appeared on coins in the guise of a lad in his teens, armored, or clothed in the consulship, first in 320, a second time in 321, a third in 324. His younger brother Constantius II became Caesar in 324; and, after the defeat of Licinius, a new title of "Augusta" glorified Helena and Fausta. With the baby Constans born in 323, the family was complete. Constantine II and Constantius II shared with their father the credit for victory over the Goths in 332. In the next year, they changed places, the former taking up duties—more accurately, apprenticeship in government—in Gaul, the latter in Syria, while Constans at last attained the rank of Caesar on Christmas Day, in the consulship of his uncle, the elder Delmatius.

In the last three years of his life, Constantine, despite the good health he continued to enjoy, began to unfold his plans for the succession. His sons' position must be made unassailable, a place secured for their cousins, the allegiance of the army directed toward its future masters. To this end, the advertisement of the Flavian princes as defenders of the northern front, winning their titles "Sarmaticus," "Gothicus," "Alamannicus," or "Germanicus," had long pointed the way. They were "The Most Noble Caesars," crowned by Victory, saluted on coins for their "Prowess" or "Providence," sharers in the celebrations of their father's anniversaries. For a decade the point had been driven home through every possible device of propaganda: Flavians were more than Constantine. A second generation stood ready to carry on. Meanwhile, however, the jealous affection of Helena had confined their cousins to a comfortable seclusion in southern France, now at Narbonne, now at Toulouse. Only after her death did Delmatius II and Hannibalianus join the court, exactly when is unknown, though their father, the elder Delmatius, appeared as consul by 333. What was to be done with them? They could neither be ignored nor put to death, not at least by Constantine, who had felt pain enough from the execution of his eldest son, Crispus. Somehow they must be incorporated into a scheme of settlement, and the future left to take care of itself. Accordingly, Hannibalianus married the princess Constantina (335) and Delmatius II became Caesar, receiving a subordinate authority over the diocese of Thrace and Macedonia and now (or in the previous year) taking command against what proved to be a merely presumptuous pretender in Cyprus.

Probably four of these five young men (excluding Hannibalianus; but other details of the matter are uncertain) had a praetorian prefect at their side, as did Constantine. Constantius II's was Ablabius, the rest obscurer names. The office had been greatly weakened during the reign, losing control of the army and of taxation, though in compensation gaining judicial authority as a court of final appeal. Ordinary procedure did not permit the emperor himself to be invoked after a prefect had spoken. Such power it was possible to surrender to the prefecture in part because it had now lost its direct hold on men and money, in part because of the multiplication of incumbents—apparently five at one time in the 330's. None of them individually constituted much of a threat to the throne. Yet the throne already prefigured a great change. It was clearly meant to rest on five legs (an almost Constantinian metaphor), namely, the three Flavian princes and their two cousins. An arrangement that scattered what had been won through such bloodshed, labor, and cost since the abdication of Diocletian, is frankly puzzling, though it does suggest

incidentally that Constantine had always desired sole rule
not for the sake of the unity of the empire but out of
personal ambition. Besides, he indicated some rank among
the heirs from which unified direction might in due course
develop. Constantine II, despite being the eldest, got the
Gallic provinces. In this and in other respects he yielded
precedence to Constantius II, given the East. Constans was
destined for Rome, Italy, Africa, and Pannonia; Delmatius
II for the Balkans, roughly speaking, and Hannibalianus
for Armenia.

This last-named region introduces events of quite a new
order. Up to 334, Constantine had had occasional diplomatic contacts with the states lying to his east, even with
India. There were Armenian campaigns of little importance
to be fought in 325, but no other action there or in upper-
most Mesopotamia, where, since Galerius' successes, a province had been formed at Persia's expense. The year 334,
however, brought the deposition of the king of Armenia
by Sapor II of Persia, who aimed to set his brother on the
vacant throne. It had been the object of centuries of inde-
cisive contention between the two super powers of the ancient world, and the settlement of 297 had accomplished
nothing more permanent than the earlier ones.

Christianity further complicated an unstable situation.
Armenia had been of that faith since a little before the
invasion by Maximin Daia (above, p. 91). It had indeed
incited that attack by the persecution of pagans, just as
Diocletian earlier had condemned an alien religion, Manichaeism, that found supporters within his own realm. As a
third instance of the same political overtones in religion:
Persia had its bishops and churches, but they were few,
whereas Rome presented in the person of Constantine and
in the eastern provinces a thoroughly and officially Chris-

tian neighbor. Persia could therefore be expected to look with suspicion on the Christians inside its own borders, and Constantine probably did not help their case by a letter he wrote to Sapor shortly after the defeat of Licinius. It opens (Eusebius gives us the text) with an ardent confession of belief.

By preserving the divine faith I partake of the light of truth; guided by the light of truth I acknowledge the divine faith. . . . Possessing the power of this God as my ally, taking my start from the furthest edges of the Ocean, I have raised the entire inhabited world, part by part, to the hopes of certain salvation. . . . On bended knees I call upon Him, fleeing from all abominable blood [–sacrifices] and odious, ill-omened smells, and turning from every earth-born flame, by which defiled, wicked and horrible error has destroyed many peoples and races.

But note the reference to "earth-born flame," striking straight at the sacred fire of the Persian state worship; note the references to "whole races" through words (*ethne, gene*) which clearly mean those beyond the empire's borders. Other paragraphs expatiate on how the true worshipper will inevitably crush all earthly enemies. Such threatening and provocative passages destroy the effect of more conciliatory appeals, at the end, for Sapor to extend his pious (!) protection to his Christian subjects. In diplomacy, Constantine is not seen at his best.

Whatever his reaction to this communication, Sapor did not turn the edge of the sword against his Christian subjects until the late 330's. But his offended faith found a more vulnerable victim in the Christian king of Armenia, whom he blinded and dethroned in 334. Armenian Christians sent an embassy to Constantine begging for help. The emperor responded by putting Constantius II in charge of operations (335), and the Romans, after preliminary reverses, defeated and killed Sapor's brother. Fighting then ceased. Late in this year or the next, Hannibalianus was given to Armenia as King of Kings, though given only by title. He made his capital a month's journey to the southwest, in Cappadocian Caesarea. Preparations to enlarge the war in a second bout went on slowly, Constantine planning to take the field in person and inviting a number of bishops to accompany the army; but an embassy arrived in the spring of 336 from Sapor, seeking peace, and Constantine acceded.

At the time, a certain Ulfilas was living at Constantinople, employed as a lector in the church. Grandson of a Cappadocian citizen whom the Goths had carried off in a raid, brought up in south Russia as one of them, and named in their tongue "Little Wolf," he came to the capital as envoy in 332. He knew Greek and Latin besides, and picked up Arianism. When he returned to the Goths as their bishop in 341, it was to carry that form of the faith among them, not in words alone, but through a Bible of which he was the translator and for which he had invented the first system of writing the Gothic language. His story continued down to much later times. Yet the early chapters coincide with the emergence of the Armenian and Persian church into the light of history, and with the spread of Christianity into the Caucasus and India through acts and saints the more miraculous for their working in such exotic lands. After the journeys of St. Paul, a second age of evangelism seemed to open in the last years of Constantine, as if the Church now had energies to lavish beyond the empire.

There is no doubt that the emperor, if he took no direct

hand in most of this activity, in his latter days felt the urge
to convert the infidel, and looked with special favor on the
entreaties of the embassy from Armenia, as he had done on
the proposals of Count Joseph, because they might both
serve the divine purpose. The letter to Sapor shows further how his mind worked. Reviewing his own extraordinary career, once more traced from its remote beginnings
to its triumphs over the whole empire (compare pp. 97
and 162), he reads into events God's inexorable power to
subdue all rulers to His servant and, thereby, to truth.
Victory in battle extended the reach of a most Christian
majesty; devoutness in his rule guaranteed an orderly kingdom. "Thus," writes Constantine to Sapor, to explain
how God governs things here on earth, "setting great
values on a just reign, He strengthens through His own
assistance and protects with the calm of peace a king who
is prudent"; or, as the poet Juvencus puts it,

Christ has granted me this peace of the age, which a benevolent
ruler of the wide-flung earth, Constantine, cherishes—with
whom, deservedly, deserved grace is present. He alone of kings
trembles at the burden of the divine title placed on him,
that, more worthy, by acts of justice, he may gain eternal
life through the ages.

Such were the ideas of the time, uniting the emperor and
his Christian subjects in a common aim and promising them
a common reward, to live in a settled, tranquil world and
by their piety during their tenancy of it to earn salvation.

Constantine was at last baptised on the eve of his death.
There was nothing unusual in delaying the sacrament so
long, in order not to lose its effects by subsequent sin; but
Constantine had put it off in hopes, too, of receiving it in
the waters of Jordan. Instead, it was to the baths of Con-

stantinople that he resorted in the spring of 337, feeling ill, and then to the hot springs of Helenopolis, where, too, the relics of the grandfather of Arianism, as we may call him—Lucian—likewise failed to make him well. He started back to the capital, getting no farther than a village on the edge of Nicomedia. There he received baptismal rites from Eusebius of that city, and there and then he discarded his purple robes to die in the white clothes of an initiate, on May 22, 337. His body was embalmed and put in a gold coffin amidst the mourning of courtiers and ministers which spread quickly into the streets, which accompanied the procession on the road westward, and soon filled Constantinople. Enormous crowds filed past the bier where it lay in state in the palace. Constantius II arrived for the burial, but the other sons did not attempt the journey.

The Church had had no occasion to establish ceremonies in honor of a deceased Christian emperor, and pagan traditions rose to the surface. A comet was duly said to have foretold Constantine's death. In a henceforward Christianized motif derived from paganism, coins depicted him drawn upwards by a hand extended from heaven. On his birthday, and on the birthday of the city that he had founded, his image received special veneration; to the statue on a porphyry column in the forum of Constantinople, Christians offered sacrifices, prayers, and incense. It was simply impossible to think of him as in any respect less than the deified emperors of paganism—his own father, or Marcus Aurelius, or any other.

A sort of paralysis descended on the empire for weeks and weeks after his death, broken by the revolt of the troops stationed in Constantinople. With or without orders, they killed Delmatius II, Hannibalianus, Ablabius, and many other members of the royal family and court. Thereafter the provisions of the emperor's will could be allowed to take effect, for Flavians only. The dynasty was loved, not its cousins; and even in the dynasty there were too many. The unprescient Eusebius had seen a proof of divine favor in Constantine's possession of three princes to succeed him; wiser men might have foretold civil war.

XII

ASSESSMENT

The title "Maximus" that a subservient senate voted Constantine in 312 had no meaning except in terms of momentary political advantage. "The Great" came to him after longer assessment at the hands of the Byzantine historians, whose reasons for making this award in part reflected merely local pride. With triumphant suddenness the center of things had been moved to a new city around which the world was to spin for ever and ever, as it seemed to them. The agent of this change deserved to be distinguished in some way fitting to the habits of his admirers. Among the Zulus, the names of special heroes became taboo; they could never be spoken again, only alluded to by periphrasis. Magniloquent Greeks had other traditions, developed under Hellenistic monarchy, taught to Rome, and transmitted to their joint heirs in the eastern half of the empire. As they looked about them from the vantage of the Golden Horn, in the fifth or sixth century, or as they reckoned distances to every point and border from the Golden Milestone, they could not doubt that the founder of Constantinople had earned whatever honor they could pay him. He was indeed Great.

In 324 Byzantium had had nine hundred years to win a place for itself among its competitors, and still ranked no higher than fiftieth, if that, among the cities of the Mediterranean. So much for inevitability! Europe funneled down to this point of land, the east-west road must traverse it, land and sea must meet before its gates; the Euxine and the Aegean touched at its harbors; but all this had been true from the beginning. Something altogether different, something or somebody beyond the ordinary was required to raise it to the fellowship of Rome and Alexandria. As a founder, Constantine belongs in the company of Romulus and Alexander. It was he that seized on the potential of the site, realizing it through such an expenditure of wealth, such a dynamic urge, such focusing of money, labor, authority, and population as the empire in its later age could not have attempted a second time.

Over the course of the century before the establishing of a new capital, the old had lost its importance. Court and ministries spent less and less time there, more and more toward the edges of the realm, where history was made—also emperors. Incumbents of the throne had a natural interest in controlling that process. Its elements were men and money, joined in an increasingly mercenary relationship. The yield of recruitment and of taxation met most often on the Danube; and if enemies sometimes threatened far away on the Rhine or Euphrates, the point equidistant between those two battle zones was, again, the lower and middle Danube. So here, experience taught, the ruler could rule best. Trèves and Antioch were too removed. Milan might do, or Nicomedia, Aquileia, Thessalonica, Serdica, Sirmium. Experiment tried them all, all were embellished with palaces, several were weighed as possibilities by Constantine, and some site in the north-central part of the empire was very clearly indicated as permanent imperial headquarters. To this extent one may speak of inevitability. But why Byzantium? Choice of that particular spot instead of any other lay with one man, perhaps also with one event. Constantine might have given his name to Sirmium, for example, if the first war with Licinius had been decisive. The subsequent course of European history would have been altered, it is impossible to say just how, but greatly. Instead, final victory came to Constantine at a point farther east, and on the Bosporus he chose to settle himself for good and all.

Founding cities was one of the things rulers did, just as today they must aspire to develop an atom bomb. It belonged to greatness. Beginning in the fourth century B.C. and entering Rome in the reign of Augustus, this fashion of display of power had dotted the map with new names of new centers or, far more frequently, of already established centers taking the name of the emperor in exchange for past or expected aid in reconstruction. Another obligation of rule was victories. The ruler must, at least ideally, undergo the same hardships as his soldiers in the field, returning to a parade in the capital. He must also patronize the arts. And day in, day out, he must submit to the demands of ceremony. In all these ways he summed up for his subjects their history and aspirations. Constantine's nephew Julian shocked people by departing from the role in the direction of naturalness and modesty. So did Marcus Aurelius, of whom we know Constantine's opinion. He called him "absurd."

In most ways, Constantine followed convention on the throne. He gives no hint of finding its formalities tedious; rather, he seems to take to them quite happily, not by suppressing any strong trait of his character—surely it would sometime have emerged—but by growing into and fulfilling expectation. Although no proof of military genius can be drawn from the high-flown descriptions of his individual campaigns, obviously he had no fear of a fight, and handled all the larger aspects—morale, supply, surprise, coordination of attack, variety of weapons—with unbroken success. Romans could be proud of their commander-in-chief, could feel that the empire was still formidable in war. In the more humdrum building of forts, noted by Constantine, as by centuries of his predecessors, with the symbol of a camp gate on his coins, tradition was maintained. He expanded the use of barbarians not in any betrayal of precedent but along lines laid down by others before him, chiefly Diocletian. He seemed to wear the uniform of the camp as easily as he did those of the court.

Many features of his policy imposed themselves on him with a force he could not control. The sign of that degree of force can be detected wherever Constantine's reign contributes neither much more nor much less than previous and succeeding ones to some steady development—for instance, the barbarization of the army and the frontier provinces. Claudius II, Constantius II, Maximian, Valentinian—they all relied heavily on Germanic troops of one tribe or another and admitted them in numbers to the empire. Their use as bodyguards was ancient, too. But the disbanding of the *equites singulares* and the praetorian guard at Rome in 312 left the honor of association with the emperor to new and decidedly barbarian *scholae palatinae*. Moreover, it was barbarians who lent themselves best to use as mobile troops. An abrupt and major redeployment under Constantine, going far beyond previous experiment, gave form to a standing army of maneuver, the *comitatenses*. Evidence suggests that this step was taken in preparation for attacks first on Maxentius and then on Licinius. Specific events thus made permanent the division between an elite corps and the territorial soldiers, the former containing a high proportion of men little or not at all

Romanised. In these changes, Constantine put his individual mark on the course of future developments.

A major trend, detectable from the beginning of the Empire but accelerated by the Tetrarchs, enlarged government as a whole but diminished its individual parts. The number of officials grew, but the various agencies, the provinces, and for that matter army units and commands, got steadily smaller. The aim was to increase the state's control over its citizens while depriving any one of them of a power base adequate to support a revolt. Constantine's reign continued this trend, but particularly affected the upper levels of administration, where the praetorian prefecture had long been dominant. Its powers were radically reduced; and those stripped from it, and others besides, were reconstituted under officials who were to remain the chief cogs in government for centuries: the various Masters, Counts, and palace officers. Their roll call includes virtually all the great ministries of the later Empire, all given a decisive shape and area of responsibility by Constantine.

What he did made sense. No doubt he must share the credit with Diocletian before him and especially with Licinius, who, at least up to 324, was simultaneously following some of the same directions as his rivals to the west. But Constantine showed real talent for administration. One proof, though much about it is obscure, was the creation of a sound gold basis on which the currency could slowly be rebuilt. Another was his handling of finances. Under Maxentius, Licinius, Diocletian, and other emperors of the time, we often hear complaints about extortionate oppression. Constantine's invention of two taxes, on senatorial landholdings and on urban commerce and crafts, hurt certain classes. On the other hand, these had been enjoying

an unfair degree of immunity; and the extremely ambitious
program of church, city, and camp construction, along
with three civil wars and the enlarging of the army, seem
to have been somehow paid for without further innovation or undue hardship. The record is a good one.

The style of rule is straightforward and practical—sometimes too much so. Treating the art of the legist as just an
obstacle between himself and the measures needed by the
age, on the impulse of fury, impatience, or kindness, he
occasionally bursts right through the ancient, wonderful
structure of Roman law. In his wilder moments he fairly
shouts at malefactors; in a calmer mood he lectures them
in the long-winded prose which rhetoricians told him
was right but which lawyers despaired of interpreting
correctly. Too moralizing, he may be carried away by his
sense of outrage; too masterful, he cannot bear to be
thwarted; too much the plain man, he distrusts what he
thinks are the tricks and pedantry of the expert in legislation. The discipline accordingly suffers permanent harm
from the style he favored.

There is something unformed and simple about it, as if
his father's background showed through. Constantius
shared with the other Tetrarchs and their immediate successors an origin in the farms, camps, and small towns of a
relatively unsophisticated society. They set the tone of
the court. Among them, ideas about slavery, physical violence, the duties of wife or son, witchcraft, higher learning—a whole range of things—differed widely from the ideas
prevailing among the older nobility, especially at Rome.
They delighted in showy titles, too, and costumes, in
crudely quantitative standards of taste; in the garish decoration or enormous size of halls and palace courtyards. In
just such matters, Constantine himself took a personal in-

terest. He gives particular directions to ensure that a church he has commissioned will offer a suitable expanse of gold across its ceiling.

If it was display he liked, then he lived in the right age. Language itself glowed like gold, and Constantine labored to acquire command at least of some tinsel glitter. Architecture unfolded new devices to astound. By Constantine they were elaborated, for example, in the palace complex at Trèves, where the audience hall still stands. The richness of the building and the form—basilical—he and his ecclesiastical advisers applied to the needs of worship with spectacular success and total disregard of cost. Exactly what part he played in decisions as to plan and dimensions, at Rome or elsewhere, is unknown—probably a minor one. What he did do was nevertheless of immense importance. He placed at the service of Pope Silvester the resources of the entire state to erect such structures as would, by their unsparing splendor and overwhelming size, serve as models to a thousand years of imitation across western Europe. Few men in history have had so great an influence on the visible world after them. And what was done at Rome was done again at Constantinople, through the octagonal Church of the Apostles, transmitting its plan to Charlemagne's chapel at Aix, or through the still grander church of Agia Sophia, begun though not completed under Constantine. The Holy Land felt his touch. Four basilicas, commemorating its most sacred sites, made of it a center for pilgrimage. To aim at immortality through stone was not peculiar only to Constantine's ambition. He was the first, however, to express the ambition as a Christian.

From his being a Christian, changes resulted in the Church and in the emperor himself.

Regarding the first, the same distinction must be made

as with the founding of Constantinople, or with any aspect
of the reign—that is, a distinction between what would, in
broad terms, have happened anyway, and what must be
attributed specifically to the intervention of Constantine.
It is conceivable, for example, that the emperor Philip
(243-249) or Gallienus (254-268) might have become a
convert. Indeed, both were said to have come close to it.
Per contra, without wrenching the truth too violently, it is
possible to imagine another two or three pagan emperors
beyond the date of 312. There is no profit in pressing such
speculations very far, but they serve to focus attention on
the fact that when a Christian first occupied the throne
and offered not only tolerance but alliance, in all the thousand ways available to him, it was at one particular junc-
ture of time—a time when the basilica stood out in people's
minds as the right and obvious shape for a place of assembly
and veneration, when the units of secular government were
reduced to a size that lent itself to use also for episcopal
sees, and when the symbolism of emperor worship and
court ceremonial were ripe for service in the portrayal of
Christ. Sarcophagus reliefs of Tetrarchic and Constantinian
times show the influence that might be exerted. Christ sits
on a throne, his feet on a footstool, exactly like the emperor. A petitioner approaches on his knees, head veiled,
exactly as to the emperor. Sometimes he offers to Christ
some gift in a hand humbly covered in a fold of his robe,
exactly according to palace usages. Or again: Sometimes in
coins of Constantius' reign and often from 325 on, the emperor's head is depicted against the background of a nimbus
(plate XIIE), and the secular model plays a decisive part
in the development of the symbol for use in later Christian
art. Illustrations could easily be multiplied to show how

one set of institutions in a certain phase of growth touched and indelibly marked another.

Synods had a history long antedating Nicaea. A large one met at Antioch in 268, others at Elvira and Ancyra quite independent of imperial initiative. The institution was developing rapidly at the period when Constantine intervened. Only another generation and it might have been strong enough to resist external patronage or control. But the idea of an ecumenical meeting emerged too early for that, under too strong a friend as ruler, and with effects influencing the course of doctrinal struggles over succeeding centuries, in which the emperors continued to summon together and influence the bishops of the Church.

Constantine seems hesitant in his dealings with the Church. Yet the impression is somewhat misleading. He was an impulsive, not overly subtle man, inclined to make decisions on inadequate grounds. When he changed his mind, as he often must do, he blamed the last previous adviser for trying to fool him, and in his anger at such wicked deceit swung to the other view the more violently. A second deficiency appeared in his makeup: an intellect not shaped for abstract argument or logical progressions. "Why couldn't people say what they meant," we can picture him wondering, "without confusing the issue?" Particularly in the Arian dispute he was at a great disadvantage in his handling of both issues and persons. Hence the tergiversations, the explosions of ill-temper, the indecisiveness which marked his policy in the 330's especially, but off and on during the previous decade as well.

Whatever he thought of his own intellectual powers, he felt no doubt about his right to influence affairs, once he was fairly involved with the Donatists—say, by 315. It would have been a brave man who challenged the emperor's presumption. Consequently the sources do not exist and probably never did exist in which relations between the Church and the throne were openly, thoroughly discussed. Things progressed by precedent and accident. At the end, though by no means as the result of Constantine's actions alone, internal struggles had become deeply secularized, both through the adoption, by competing parties, of the tone and devices of ordinary political strife, and through the thrust of the imperial will into their midst. Some attempt shows in Eusebius to define a position for his eminent friend, whose genuine devoutness he felt sure of and whose readiness to defend, advance, and enrich Christianity he could not praise enough; but the closest approach to a solution may have been Constantine's own description of himself as "bishop of those outside the Church." It suggested, quite accurately, that he would not vote in councils, would not absolutely impose his doctrine on others, and would not presume to excommunicate anyone. At most he would make secular authority available to enforce decisions by the orthodox.

"Bishop of those outside the Church" suggested also a sense of mission. Evidence for this is abundant and conclusive. Constantine promoted the spread of Christianity beyond the frontiers, still more within them. He tried to reclaim heretics and schismatics. His motive, however, was not to save souls but, one may almost say, bodies. He aimed at the prosperity of his reign and realm through ensuring to God acceptable worship, and by prosperity he evidently had in mind quite material well-being: an end to civil war, security along the borders, plentiful crops for a plentiful population—in short, peace and its products. An idea of God's gifts is reflected in the evils that Constantine laid at the Devil's door: rioting, strife in the streets, bitter dispute, bad harvests, pretenders, and all the works of witchcraft. One must adjust one's expectations of the effects of conversion to the man and the age.

Few of the essential elements of Christian belief interested Constantine very much—neither God's mercy nor man's sinfulness, neither damnation nor salvation, neither brotherly love nor, needless to say, humility. Ardent in his convictions, he remained nevertheless oblivious to their moral implications. Modern historians have been bothered by this; ancient pagans turned it to good account. According to their stories, the emperor experienced no change of faith until after he had put to death his son and wife, whereupon he sought for purification from the old gods. Denied it by their lofty justice, he resorted to Christianity, through which he obtained a spurious substitute. Retribution at last caught up with him. His brothers poisoned him in revenge for the killing of Crispus.

Through such stories, pagans of the fifth or sixth century snarled at the dead Constantine and snapped around his heels. But "Greatest," Maximus, or merely Great, he was above the reach of their malice.

BIBLIOGRAPHICAL NOTE

Arduum est res gestas scribere (Sallust)
"History is hard work."

The sources of our knowledge about Constantine are both written and unwritten. The latter (let me add inscriptions, illogically) include the vestiges of buildings, the milestones, chance works of art, and coins that have been discovered, and which in total contribute a great deal of information of a type generally missing in the written sources; but they are treated in a literature too technical and scattered to be of much use to the general reader.

Written sources for this period, in contrast to those for the century preceding, are relatively abundant. The majority have been translated. The panegyrics, most of the accounts of the persecutions in the form of martyrs' Acts, a few late (fifth century on) Church historians, and parts of the dossier of Donatism and Arianism, do not exist in English; but the rest, making up four-fifths of the total, do. Roughly in order of importance, they are to be found in the two series, the Ante-Nicene Fathers, and the Nicene and Post-Nicene Fathers (Eusebius, Lactantius, and others); in J. Stevenson, *A New Eusebius* (1963), an imaginative, sensible collection that opens doors onto many less-known writers; in *The Theodosian Code*, trans. by C.

Pharr and others (1952); in the first volume of P. R. Cole-
man-Norton, *Roman State and Christian Church* (1966);
and in Zosimus, *Historia Nova*, trans. by J. J. Buchanan
and H. T. Davis (1967). Even some of the obscurest or
most tangential are available: the so-called Anonymous
Valesianus tacked on to the third volume of Ammianus
Marcellinus in the Loeb Library series (1952), or Eunapius'
Lives of the Philosophers in the same series. But by this
point in the list, the returns for a student of Constantine
are quite minor.

The bulk of the written material is by Christians about
Christianity, thus strongly illuminating one side of Constantine's character and life but leaving another in deep
shadow. Modern scholars usually submit to this balance of
light, rightly if they are studying the reign as an important
episode in the history of the Church, wrongly if they are
studying it on its own terms and for its own sake.

A scholar well up on the subject mentions in 1950 that
he had compiled for his own purposes a bibliography of
more than fifteen hundred books and articles in learned
journals—a depressing statistic; and of course many more
titles of capital interest have been added in the nearly
twenty years since then. Constantinian studies are an inter-
national possession, almost a passion, one might suppose,
from the quantity of good work done in German, French,
and Italian. The items in English, however, are unfortunately extremely few, though of high quality. First I would
mention A. H. M. Jones' excellent *Constantine and the
Conversion of Europe* (1948), intended for much the same
purpose and on the same scale as the present work, though
offering different slants. Next, perhaps, N. H. Baynes'
beautifully balanced short essay, *Constantine the Great and
the Christian Church* (Proceedings of the British Academy

XV, and separately published, 1929). A. Alföldi's *The Conversion of Constantine and Pagan Rome* (1948) is extraordinarily vivid and penetrating—really dangerously persuasive on arguable points; and J. Burckhardt's classic, *The Age of Constantine the Great* (1852; translated, like the preceding, from German) is almost equally vigorous, though insensitive to the spirit of the times and to the spirit of Constantine. Two recent collections of essays should be mentioned, scholarly and narrowly focused but not forbiddingly technical: volume XXI of the *Dumbarton Oaks Papers* (1967) and *The Conflict Between Paganism and Christianity in the Fourth Century* (ed. by A. Momigliano, 1963). They offer access, through their footnotes, to a representative range of the technical literature. For a broader look at things, the standard larger treatment is the last volume of the *Cambridge Ancient History* (1939) and the first volume of the *Cambridge Medieval History* (1911), though between the two of them they somehow forget early Arianism and several other topics. A shorter account can be found in the first half of J. Vogt, *The Decline of Rome* (1965; Eng. trans., 1967).

INDEX